Contents

KT-527-329

The opening screen on the WordPress Dashboard fits a lot of information onto the screen. You can drag and drop the various widgets (small apps), expand and compress them and remove them by using **Screen Options**.

The **Side Panel Menu** gives you access to all areas of the WordPress installation. You can dismiss all the messages that will accumulate in the **Message Area**. The **Login Option** lets you update your profile including a colour scheme for the dashboard.

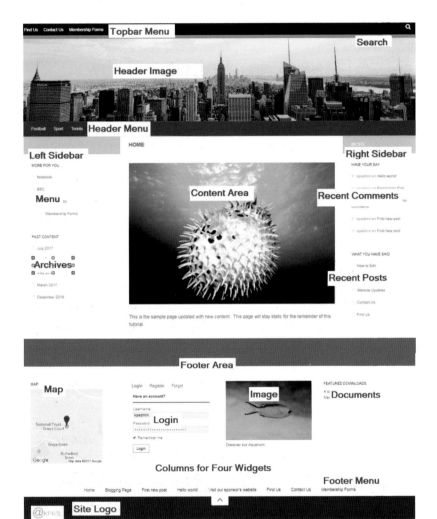

A more complicated WordPress website with two **Sidebars**, four **Menus**, a **Header Image** and a lot of detail in the **Footer Area**. In this design the **Site Logo** is at the very bottom of the website.

1

WordPress and Website Basics

WordPress is a software tool to create a website without the need to have an in-depth knowledge of how the pages are put together. It is developed by a community of very talented programmers and is released for use under an open-source licence. This type of licence lets website builders use the core software for free and on as many websites as they like.

WordPress is used on about 30% of all the websites on the internet, around 80 million and rising. WordPress is classed as a Content Management System or CMS. A CMS has a template or theme to style and format the content correctly for the web browser. The CMS software wraps the content with all the other tags and code needed to display the content in the web browser.

There are many other CMS tools, such as Drupal and Joomla, and they all try to provide the website creator with an easy-to-use editor to quickly create a professional looking website. Each of the leading CMS tools has their fans but WordPress has become one of the easier ones to learn and extend.

The core software is free to use but many companies and individuals make a living by creating themes and additional software modules to enhance the WordPress package.

Fig. 1.1 The WordPress site is a valuable reference for any questions or general information.

A search on the internet for WordPress will likely list *https://wordpress.com* at the top of the retrieval list. This is the commercial arm of WordPress and the website that contains support information is located at *https://wordpress.org.*

Fig. 1.2 The NBA in the USA uses WordPress as listed under the showcase tab of the Wordpress.org website.

The Themes tab displays the wide variety of **templates** or **themes** available for WordPress. At this stage just view them as possibilities as the developers tailor them to look their best. It is best to create a WordPress website using one of the themes installed with the core software as they tend to work best with add-ons.

The **Plugins** tab lists many of the add-ons or additional modules available for WordPress. There is generally a plugin to do nearly everything you might want but they come with a warning that a lot of time can be wasted on trying to get plugins to work as expected. There is another type of add-on software called **Widgets** that are like mini-plugins but very useful nonetheless.

Building a Website

I recommend working your way through the book chapter by chapter even if you skip a few pages here and there. The learning stages are:

The Internet	Understand some necessary terminology so that you can buy hosting and/or WordPress. It also helps you interact with support teams
WordPress	Install your WordPress based website using one of the options.
WordPress Dashboard	Use the dashboard to secure your website , create pages, posts , categories and tags.
WordPress Editor	Editor functions and extend the basic editor.
WordPress Theme	Customise one of the supplied themes, choose a new one, enable widgets and menus.
Plugins	Add functionality using selected plugins. Newsletters, Maps, Contact forms.
Appendices	The more technical stuff covering the easiest ways to install WordPress.

Mobile WordPress

WordPress for iOS

WordPress for iOS is the app that lets you write posts, upload photos, edit pages, and manage comments on your blog from your iPhone, iPad, or iPod touch. With support for both self-hosted WordPress (3.6 or higher) and WordPress.com, users of all experience levels can get going in seconds.

WordPress for Android

Write new posts for your WordPress blog, edit content, and manage comments with built-in notifications, all on your Android device.

Learn more | Download

A desktop app that gives WordPress a permanent home in your taskbar.

DOWNLOAD THE APP:

WINDOWS (7+)

Fig. 1.3 WordPress promotes the apps for Android and iOS but there is also one for Windows mobile devices. The apps provide an alternative to using a browser.

Web Servers

Modern websites appear to be very complicated with many visual effects aimed to capture and keep the attention of the casual visitor. Behind the scenes, they are just a collection of files in folders and Fig. 1.4 lists the files and folders that make up a WordPress installation.

Filename	Size	Date		Permissions
<..>				
..				
wp-admin		05/24/17	13:55	drwxr-xr-x
wp-content		05/24/17	14:21	drwxr-xr-x
wp-includes		01/11/17	13:35	drwxr-xr-x
.htaccess	241	12/06/16	00:00	-rw-r--r--
index.php	418	09/25/13	00:00	-rw-r--r--
license.txt	19 KB	01/14/17	14:18	-rw-r--r--
readme.html	7 KB	05/17/17	05:06	-rw-r--r--
wp-activate.php	5 KB	01/11/17	13:35	-rw-r--r--
wp-blog-header.php	364	12/19/15	00:00	-rw-r--r--
wp-comments-post.php	1 KB	01/11/17	13:35	-rw-r--r--
wp-config-sample.php	2 KB	12/16/15	00:00	-rw-r--r--
wp-config.php	2 KB	12/06/16	00:00	-rw-r--r--

Fig. 1.4 Various file and folders on a web host.

WordPress prefixes many of the files with **wp-**. The files are stored on a remote computer called a **web server**, so called because it serves up files to other computers devices. Another name for this server is a **web host** and companies that provide these services are known as **web hosting companies**. The web server sends these files in a logical sequence to the browser software on users' devices and the browser uses this data to create the web pages. Web hosting companies offer both Linux or Windows based web servers and if offered a choice pick the Linux option. If you opt to use a managed solution then you can leave all of the technical stuff to the web hosting company.

Web Browsers

It is the browser software like Chrome or Safari that interprets the data sent to the PC or tablet to create or render the web pages on the website. You will also use your browser to create and update your WordPress website. It is therefore important to understand them in a little more detail and to know how to check that they are as up-to-date as possible.

Fig. 1.5 Identify the browsers by their icons. Left to right they are Firefox, Internet Explorer (IE), Safari and Chrome.

Browsers are now more consistent in the way they interpret codes and data from the remote server than in the past but there are still occasions when a web page will behave oddly in one browser and not in another. For that reason and for information security it is important to keep your browser software up-to-date. Many of them have monthly updates.

There are many browsers available but it is likely that you will be using one from the top four providers as shown in Figure 1.5. It is worth considering using one browser for WordPress and another for general activities such as online banking where it is very important that any add-on security software such as Trusteer (Rapport) is not disabled temporarily by a browser update. With some browsers the mere act of checking for an update can actually launch an update that you cannot undo.

Chrome, Firefox and Safari are available for most devices and for the most part behave identically on Android, Apple and Windows 7, 8 and 10.

Microsoft is the exception with two browsers. Internet Explorer (IE) that reached the end of life (not updated by Microsoft) with Windows 7.   IE is available on Android. The Microsoft Edge browser is only available   on Windows 10 and is evolving quickly with the list of add-on software called extensions growing.

Google Chrome

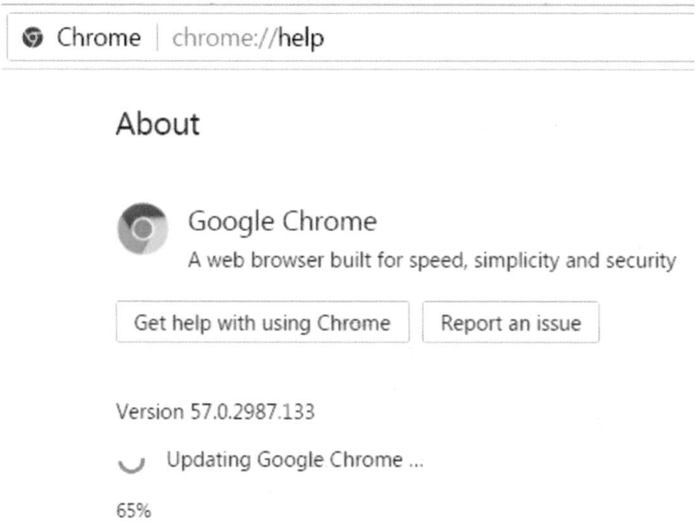

Fig. 1.6 The option to update Chrome is found at Settings -> Help -> About Google Chrome. Opening this menu item will trigger an update if one is pending.

Chrome on Windows doesn't update itself automatically so it is possible to get way behind with the most up-to-date version. It is worth checking for updates every month by going to the customisation menu (the three vertical dots) in the top right corner of the screen and choosing the *About Google Chrome* option. This launches the update checking option that might need a reboot to complete the installation.

On Android and Apple, Chrome updates automatically if your general settings allow it. It is often a better to disallow automatic updates and update applications manually.

Firefox

This browser keeps track of updates and implements them when you open it up provided it is set up to do that.

Fig. 1.7 Location of settings in Firefox.

To check how updates occur open the Settings menu (three horizontal lines) and select Options. Next choose Advanced and then the Update tab. The automatic update is the best option but if you prefer to be in control of updates then option 2 is OK as well (Figure 1.8).

You can also check when the last update was applied by clicking on the Update History as shown in Figure 1.9.

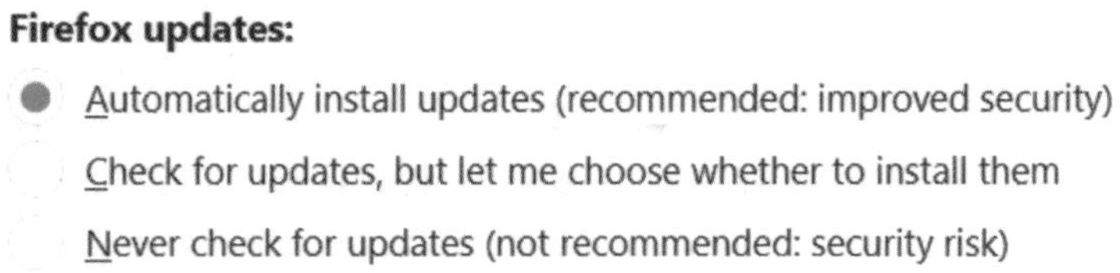

Firefox updates:

● Automatically install updates (recommended: improved security)

○ Check for updates, but let me choose whether to install them

○ Never check for updates (not recommended: security risk)

Fig. 1.8 The Firefox update options.

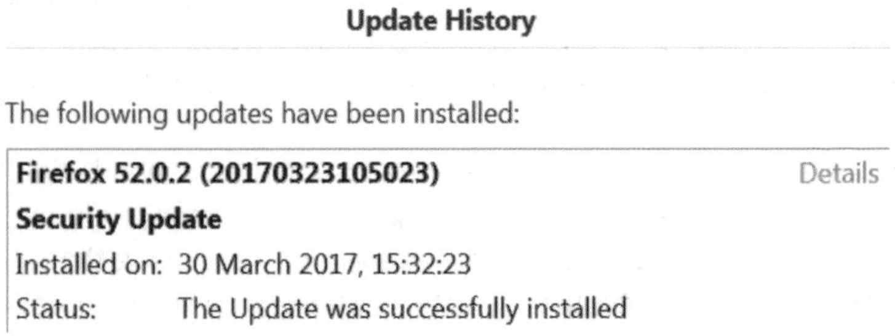

Update History

The following updates have been installed:

Firefox 52.0.2 (20170323105023)   Details
Security Update
Installed on: 30 March 2017, 15:32:23
Status: The Update was successfully installed

Fig. 1.9 Update History shows details of the last security update.

On Android and Apple, Firefox will update automatically if the device's general settings allow it. If not the updates are flagged in **Apple's App store** and the **Google Play** app store.

Internet Explorer (IE)

Fig. 1.10 Internet Explorer 11 version information obtained from the settings menu entry About Internet Explorer.

IE is now regarded by Microsoft to be a legacy browser and any updates will now be triggered by a serious security breach. New internet coding standards will not be implemented and web pages may exhibit some strange effects.

IE11 was the last version for Windows 8 and below and is tightly tied to those versions of the Windows operating system. It is possible to get a version of IE for Windows 10 by opening the Edge browser and opting to use IE instead of Edge. This is a special version of IE that Microsoft will likely keep secure.

The internet is full of suggestions on how to run IE10 on Android, a version that is well out of date. It is best to avoid them as they will lead to confusing results.

IE is not available on Apple directly but depending on the version of Safari installed on the iMac the User Agent link in the **Develop** menu

Fig. 1.11 Open the Develop tab for any IE emulators included with Safari.

may have an IE emulator of some kind. This feature is not available on some mobile devices. Please read the section on Safari before trying to find a version to download.

Microsoft Edge

This browser appeared with Windows 10 release and is the one Microsoft wants you to use with that version of the operating system.   The slightly different logo is a quick way to tell it apart from IE. Edge is only available on Windows 10 and will not install on any other version of their operating system.   Microsoft stated a while ago that Edge is exclusive to Windows and there will not be a version for Android or iOS.

Edge works fully when logged into a Microsoft online account, something you might not want to do. The browser gives you little information about its update status as it forms part of the general Windows update.

Safari

Apple is close to restricting Safari to just Apple devices after a period of trying to make it available on the Android and Windows operating systems. Any non-iOS versions should be treated as a security risk and any websites offering downloads are to be

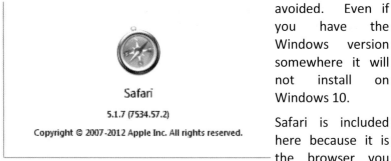

Safari

5.1.7 (7534.57.2)

Copyright © 2007-2012 Apple Inc. All rights reserved.

Fig. 1.12 The last version of Safari for Windows 7 and XP/Vista.

avoided. Even if you have the Windows version somewhere it will not install on Windows 10.

Safari is included here because it is the browser you will most likely use on your iOS device.

Other Browsers

There are many more browsers to choose from such as Opera, available on most operating systems or Dolphin on Android and Windows and all of them will work when setting up a WordPress website. If you are familiar with a particular browser then continue to use it unless you have a problem.

Browser Interaction

Browsers don't interact with each other now, so you can safely install more than one on your device. You may get annoying messages as each one tries to become the default browser but there is usually a tick box to stop this happening. You can change your default browser at any time to make it the new default. Usually this is on the first page of the Settings or Options.

Choice of Browser

A browser is almost a personal choice but when creating a WordPress website consider having at least one other browser on your device. Your website users will have different browsers and the website must work as well as possible on each one, otherwise a warning is needed to alert users to which browser works best.

Some users will have out-of-date browsers and there is very little you can do about that. They will be having problems on many other websites.

Google Chrome is a good first choice for Windows and Android followed by Firefox as they are both updated on a regular basis. Safari is your first choice for iOS on Apple devices.

There is unlikely to be a problem with the core WordPress software and any issues will be caused by the theme or a piece of additional software.

Website Basics

Like many aspects of the computing world , the internet has its own terminology.   There are a handful of terms that a WordPress user needs to know so that they can set up the website correctly.

http and https

Most of us are used to seeing website addresses starting with *http://www* indicating that you are viewing a *regular* website basically for information. It also means that all the data passing between your browser and the website is in the clear and is without any encryption to jumble up the data packets.

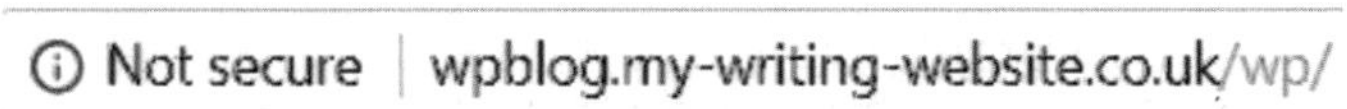

ⓘ Not secure | wpblog.my-writing-website.co.uk/wp/

Fig. 1.13 Chrome's way of telling you that this is not a secure website. It may not matter but can worry some users.

Websites that start with *https://www* use a technique called SSL, or Secure Sockets Layer, to encrypt or encode the data

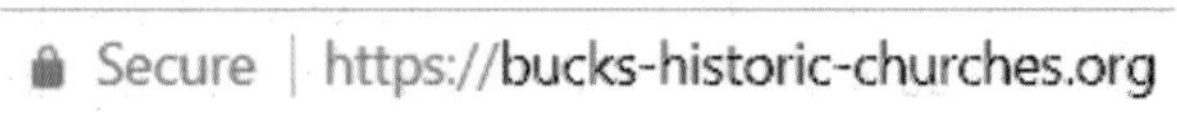

🔒 Secure | https://bucks-historic-churches.org

Fig. 1.14 Chrome flags a secure website with encrypted data in green letters.

between the browser and the website.

These websites issue a **security certificate** to the browser from a recognised issuer like Verisign. The internet browser will alert you if a website is using a certificate it doesn't recognise usually advising you not to proceed. You need to judge if this is possibly a security risk. You can add the website to an exception list by following the link offered by the browser.

For a club, church or members' website going to the expense of acquiring a valid certificate and renewing it each year is generally not necessary. However, browsers are alerting users to any site that is not operating in https mode and that can alarm website administrators and users.

When you purchase web space from a hosting company they usually attach an **SSL certificate** of their own as **self-certification**, which was acceptable for many years. This trend is changing.

Web browsers now expect to see a certificate from a known provider. The prices continue to fall so SSL certificates can cost as little as £35 per annum or may even come as part of a hosting contract. You will see later that some of the larger hosting providers offer SSL/https at a minimal or at no extra cost.

Using http://www or just http://

There is another trend towards dropping the *www* part of the domain name and most modern web browsers can cope with that.

However, strictly two URLs of the form http:// www.domain.co.uk and http://domain.co.uk are different websites. The web hosting company binds the various versions of the domain together to point at the same website on the web server so it is usually not a worry. Sometimes the hosting provider only offers one or other version.

Domain Names

Domain names have a hierarchy of their own called a Domain Name System (DNS) and the most familiar Top Level Domains (TLD) are two letter ISO country codes. The TLD for the UK is *.uk* and then the next level is added such as *.co.uk* and then a unique name such as *bbc* completes a domain of bbc.co.uk.

The DNS was overhauled recently to expand it and a full explanation and listing of around 1,000 TLDs can be found at https://www.iana.org/domains/root/db/

Internet Assigned Numbers Authority

Fig. 1.15 There is a lot of Information about domain names on this website.

You also find domains with a generic TLD like *.com*, *.org* and *.net*. There are guidelines on using these and a few organisations ignore them.

The *.com* is for commercial entities that sell stuff, like an online store and it originated in the USA, *.org* can be used by charities and *.net* is for companies providing internet services. These gTLDs are more expensive than .co.uk so stick with the latter if you can.

More specialized TLDs are being offered to the creators of websites such as .technology and .radio and might be something to consider if you will be in a niche market.

Choosing a Domain Name

Choosing a domain name may take some time especially if the first choice has been taken. As stated above try to stay with the most common local domain name suffix. This will be .co.uk or simply .uk in the UK , .ie for Ireland or .ca for Canada. It helps to create a list of possible domain names that reflect the organisation's activities, purpose or location.

Obtaining a Domain Name

There are many companies that can suggest and lodge or register your domain name with the central registry to prevent others using the same name (Figure 1.16). A domain name is an easier way for humans to remember a website's address that computers store as a number like 103.456.545.237. This number is called the IP address.

It is a good idea to purchase space on a website host at the same time as registering a domain name as they will set it all up and send the details in an e-mail.

Fig. 1.16 A typical domain search box.

The internet works on credit or debit cards and possibly PayPal so be prepared for that. I am not aware of very many hosting companies that will invoice you and accept a cheque these days.

The internet usually updates the DNS records in a few minutes but it can take 48 hours for your website to appear in a browser mainly due to the lag in updating secondary DNS servers. If the website is still not accessible after two days then raise a support ticket with your web host or refer to the troubleshooting guide in Appendix 4 to change your DNS provider to either Google or OpenDNS. The appendix covers Windows, Apple and Android.

WordPress as a Package

The preceding pages were written as a basic guide to the components that make the internet work the way it does. It is there as a reference to help you make the correct choices when purchasing hosting space and also to give you confidence if you have to deal with technical support people who sometimes assume that you have a certain level of knowledge.

Action Points

The points to take away and think about from this chapter concern the domain name of your website and whether it needs to be http or https.

Before searching for your preferred domain using a provider like 123Reg. Using a fictitious entity the provider listed four typical and 27 other variants using the new TLDs. (Figure 1.17).

Search results (4)

✔ brigstonunited.CO.UK

✔ brigstonunited.UK

✔ brigstonunited.UK.COM

✔ brigstonunited.UK.NET

Fig. 1.17 The top four domain names suggested by 123Reg.

Search results (4)

✖ imperialcafe.CO.UK

✖ imperialcafe.UK

✔ imperialcafe.UK.COM

✔ imperialcafe.UK.NET

A more common search for a café name like *The Imperial* gives less choice so think about adding the location either as a compound word or by putting hyphens in between.

Fig. 1.18 A more common name will likely find the domain already registered.

The second thing to think about is whether you need a secure website. There are two considerations. You might need a secure website because your business will benefit from displaying the secure symbol in the users' web browsers. Secondly your users may get worried if their browsers flag up security errors and most casual users are unlikely to know how to tell their browsers to trust a particular website.

Adding an SSL option to make your website secure is more easily done on a clean installation and will probably be cheaper.

Finding the Best Solution

Searching the internet will give you a list of many companies that can provide what you want. I tend to avoid these and use those websites that review how good the major providers are in a particular year. Two of my favourites are shown below but make sure that you are reading the UK or local editions of their publications.

Fig. 1.19 Two of the best websites for reviews of all types of internet services.

PC Magazine is widely available in shops and on newsstands. Their website provides reviews of many products and services needed to build a website. Techradar is highly regarded.

Use them as a guide but make your final choice based on your own research.

2

WordPress Overview

 WordPress is classed as a Content Management System or CMS, meaning that users focus on adding content and not on coding the framework of the website. WordPress is used by millions of users and has an active development community. The core software is free and many companies sell enhancements known as plugins or new website templates known as themes. WordPress is updated on a regular basis and the dashboard lists all available updates.

The key features are shown in Figure 2.1 below. Website builders have little control over **SEO** (Search Engine Optimisation) **Friendly** settings, **High Performance** and **High Security**. **Customizable Designs** and **Responsive Mobile Sites**

Fig. 2.1 The key features of WordPress as defined by WordPress.org.

are part of the template for the site.   The top feature is **Powerful   Media** (I think that it should really say Content Management). There is a lot of information on the WordPress website about the system in a repository called the **Codex** but it is written from a technical perspective and it can be difficult to work out whether it is important or not.

WordPress is a piece of blogging software, a location on the internet to record information in a timeline and is widely used for this purpose by individuals and business. In a blog, new information, called posts, displaces old information on the timeline but that is not always the best way to do things.

By selecting a single option WordPress can become a *static website* where the website editor controls the content of the web pages. Static doesn't mean that content can't be edited or replaced.

Installing WordPress

There are several ways to get your website up and running and the path chosen will depend on individual computer skills and how you want to make things happen. For example, users who enjoy learning new things and want to really understand how a website functions might opt for a more hands-on method. Alternatively, if you want to just get going creating content as quickly as possible then one of the hosted solutions is probably the best answer.

The various options are summarised on the following pages with the details in a corresponding appendix. The examples detailed in the appendix for options 2 and 3 are based on just one of many providers. They were chosen as a result of the author's own positive experiences of using their processes and his interaction with the company's support teams. These can change over time so do use some caution before jumping in.

Option 1 - WordPress.com

This is a relatively easy one to follow, a case of carefully choosing options and the basic level of computer knowledge needed is covered in chapter 1.

Fig. 2.2 WordPress.com is a very quick way to get your all-in-one solution.

WordPress offers a web hosting service of its own aimed at both the novice and high-end business. Plans start at free where the website users have to accept adverts to about £25-£30 per month for business. Prices are in dollars and will vary with the exchange rate.

This option integrates with the WordPress app available for Windows, Android and Apple that makes management of the website a lot easier. More information is contained in Appendix 1.

Option 2 - Hosting Company

Fig. 2.3 This hosting company may include an SSL certificate for free.

This option uses an alternative hosting provider but works very much like the WordPress.com setup and is about the same level of difficulty provided you just work through your browser.

You can add your website to the WordPress app but it can be a little fiddly. There are many providers in the field and you need to carry out some research to find the best provider for you. More information is contained in Appendix 2.

Option 3 - Install by Script

This is a little more difficult in that it is in two stages.

Fig. 2.4 Pickaweb provides a good range of hosting solutions.

Users buy the hosting space first, set it up to their requirements and then install WordPress using the provider's application store. Here a little bit more knowledge of websites is needed but it certainly gives you a lot more control.

More information in Appendix 3 but note that you will need to spend more time finding your away around different interfaces.

Option 4 - DIY Method

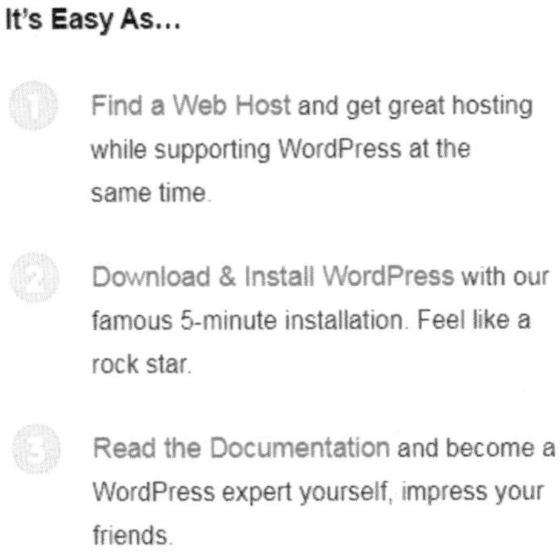

It's Easy As...

1. Find a Web Host and get great hosting while supporting WordPress at the same time.

2. Download & Install WordPress with our famous 5-minute installation. Feel like a rock star.

3. Read the Documentation and become a WordPress expert yourself, impress your friends.

This is the complete DIY option and is more difficult to do mainly because several extra software tools are required to unpack (unzip) the WordPress files, create the underlying database and upload the suite of files to the web server.

It is not recommended as part of an easy guide to create a website using WordPress.

Fig. 2.5 WordPress makes it sound easy but does not tell you how much you need to know.

3

WordPress Dashboard

WordPress has a control panel called the *dashboard* and this chapter explores the dashboard of a native WordPress website. This means that it has not been modified by WordPress.com or a hosting company where some of the settings are removed or greyed out. For the most part, the various dashboards are very similar so this chapter is a general guide to all variants.

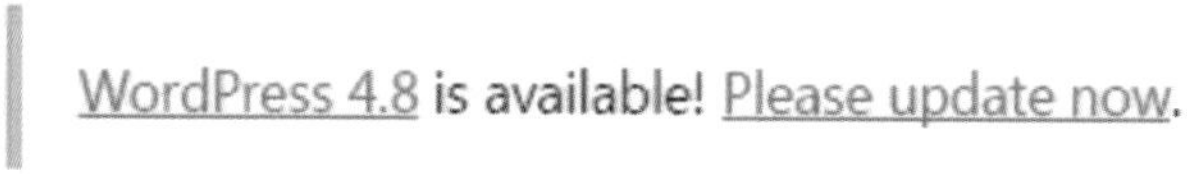

WordPress 4.8 is available! Please update now.

Fig. 3.1 WordPress always flags you when an update is available.

When logging in as the **site administrator** or admin it is normal to see messages (Figure 3.1) to perform certain actions that are mainly about updates or adding additional software modules. Some messages come from themes or plugins (Figure 3.2) and some from the application itself.

Image Widget Plus - Add lightbox, slideshow, and random image widgets. Find out how!

Fig. 3.2 A plugin trying to attract your attention. Many messages are to encourage you to upgrade to paid products.

It is unlikely that any messages will have to be actioned immediately so wait to get more familiar with WordPress before accepting some or all of them.

Logging in

To login into WordPress enter the URL that either WordPress.com or the hosting company provided as part of the setup process into your browser address bar .

The general form of a WordPress login is:

http://www.mywebsite.co.uk/wp/wp-login.php

Look for a similar, but it probably won't be exactly the same, URL in the documentation gathered during the website creation stage.

C   ⓘ Not secure | wpblog.my-writing-website.co.uk/wp/wp-login.php

Fig. 3.3 The admin login from one of the author's websites.

Welcome to WordPress!

We've assembled some links to get you started:

Get Started

Customize Your Site

or, change your theme completely

Fig. 3.4 The WordPress welcome screen.

Once logged in to your admin area you should expect to see this (Figure 3.4) greeting from WordPress. It is an indication that all is well with your website.

Side Panel Menu

All the WordPress settings are in the concertina style side menu. If other options are available the menu expands to the right with those options. Simply click on a menu item to see what is

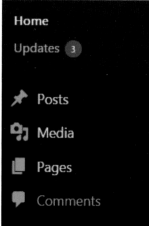

Fig. 3.5 Part of the WP dashboard on the left side of the admin area.

available. On the left, under the expanded menu item, will be an option, labelled **Collapse menu**, to collapse the menu when you are finished.

The sidebar also shows the updates that are available by a number in a coloured circle typically orange or blue (Figure 3.5).

A sensible approach is to work with a policy of waiting a week or more before installing updates just in case the theme or plugin has errors. WordPress does not have an easy way to roll back or uninstall upgrades to itself or to installed plugins.

The Menu Item by Item

The WordPress menu is the heart of the website and knowing what it contains can save a lot of time in the future. The sidebar menu items are explained in order of their importance

Settings –General

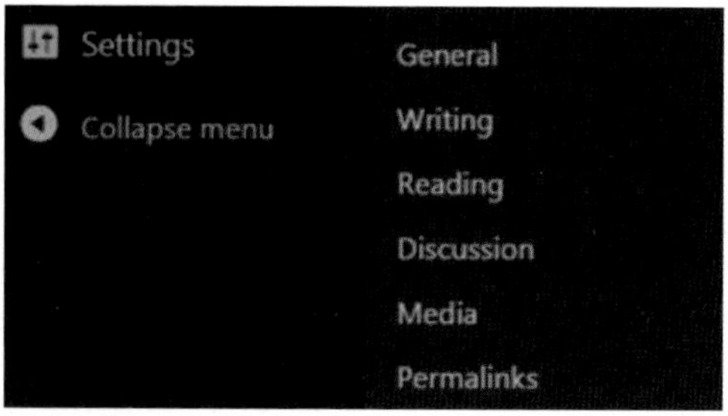

Fig. 3.6 The expanded Settings menu.

Click on the General link to open that sub menu (Figure 3.6). Starting from the top down, look for Site Title and Tagline (Figure 3.7).

At first glance these settings seem to be independent of each other but they need to be considered together so that the purpose of your website is displayed correctly. The content in the boxes is not fixed and can be changed as many times as is necessary.

Site Title   My Blog

Tagline   My WordPress Blog

Fig. 3.7 Site and Tagline settings.

The Site Title and the Tagline both appear on the home page and it provides important information for both human visitors and search engines.

Fig. 3.8 This is how the Hueman theme displays the site title and tagline on a web page.

How the words are displayed is governed by the theme that should always display them. The only thing that might stop this is that some themes overwrite the Site Title words if a logo is added to the site. If the active theme will display it the Tagline text appears below or to the right of the Site Title (Figure 3.8). Other themes will put the Tagline underneath the Site Title and very rarely ignore it completely

`<title>My Blog - My WordPress Blog</title>`

Fig. 3.9 The Site Title and the Tagline are encoded and is an important piece of data used by all the major search engines.

Even if the theme doesn't display the Tagline, it is an important piece of information as WordPress concatenates the information together to form the site title HTML tag (Figure 3.9).

Search engines use this tag and you will see it appear in the search engines search results (Figure 3.10).

My Blog – My WordPress Blog - my-writing-website.co.uk
wpblog.my-writing-website.co.uk/wp/ ▾
This is the sample page updated with new content. This page will stay static for the tutorial. GET A NO RISK, FREE CONSULTATION TODAY.

Fig. 3.10 Google likes to display the title HTML tag information.

WordPress URL and Site URL

It is important not to change these settings as just a single letter change could catastrophically damage your website to the extent that it may be extremely difficult to login into it (Figure 3.11).

There is a link to the WordPress codex, the technical reference work, that you can visit to see for yourself how complex this is and in general there is no need to change anything.

WordPress Address (URL)   `http://wpblog.my-writing-website.co.uk/wp`

Site Address (URL)   `http://wpblog.my-writing-website.co.uk/wp`

Fig. 3.11 URL and Site URL settings should not be changed.

E-mail Address

This can be changed at will and as many times as you need to so long as it contains a valid e-mail address available to the administrator.

Membership

This setting is in two parts. By ticking the *Anyone can register* (Figure 3.12) box it allows the people to register on the website and a Register link will appear on one of the menus (Figure 3.13).

Membership   ✔ Anyone can register

New User Default Role   Subscriber   ▾

Fig. 3.12 Two settings that control access to web pages.

Register For This Site

Fig 3.13 Ticking the box allows anyone, human or spambot
to register on your website and that is not a good
thing to allow.

Visitors clicking on this link (Figure 3.13—Register for This Site) on the web get a registration screen simply asking for a user name and password.

Until a policy has been set on users leave the box (**Anyone can register**) unticked as the administrator email may get flooded

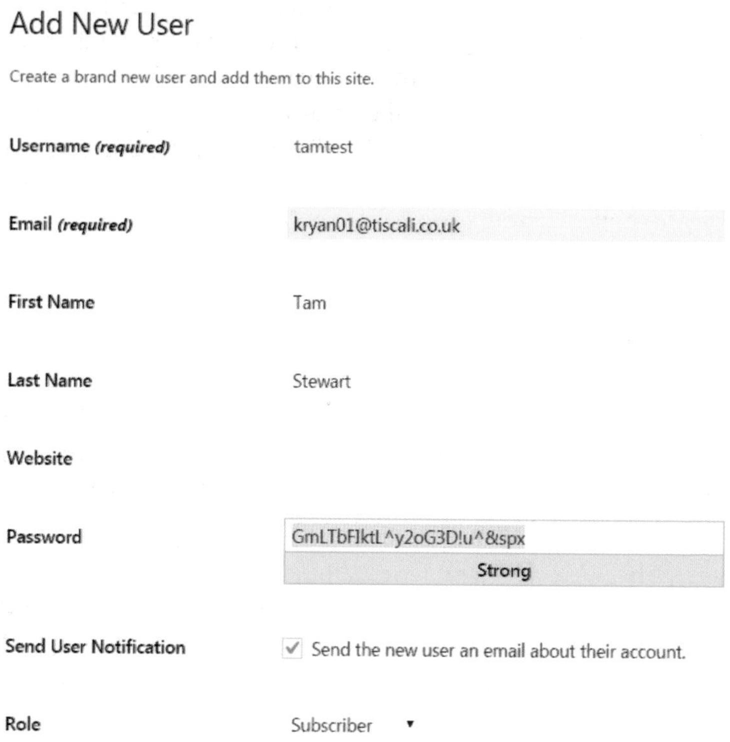

Add New User

Create a brand new user and add them to this site.

Username *(required)*	tamtest
Email *(required)*	kryan01@tiscali.co.uk
First Name	Tam
Last Name	Stewart
Website	
Password	GmLTbFJktL^y2oG3D!u^&spx
	Strong
Send User Notification	✓ Send the new user an email about their account.
Role	Subscriber ▼

Fig. 3.14 The Add New User screen is how you can add users manually.

with messages from unknown companies offering WordPress development services. Allowing registration may be a useful feature for a website if there is public content and information restricted to members but you need to put other controls in place.

If you need other people involved in your website project before it is ready for public use then add these users manually (Figure 3.14) as it gives you control over passwords and then they can login using the same URL as you use for the admin login. They only get access to the functions you give them via their user **Role**.

There are five Role types from simple access to administrator level access. All the users, irrespective of their permissions are controlled by the administrator who can add, delete and downgrade/upgrade them. When the administrator adds users and issue passwords to them WordPress tries to enforce very strong passwords as shown in Figure 3.14 and if at all possible use the suggested passwords as a way to enforce site security.

Subscriber

This is the lowest level available and is a user who has an account but can only manage their own profile. A user profile is a very simple record consisting of their name, a public name and a place to add some limited general personal details. The profile is viewable by other users on the site so users should only include personal details they are happy for others to see.

When this type of user logs in they can change the colour scheme of their profile, not the website itself, and all their personal information except the username. The public name is controlled by WordPress and only a number of variations are allowed.

Contributor

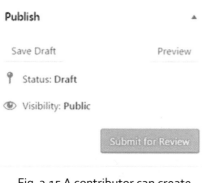

Fig. 3.15 A contributor can create articles but cannot publish them .

This is the next level up and a contributor can write and manage their own posts but they cannot publish them. They are collected with the published posts and pages and can only be released to the website by another user who has permission to do so.

The site administrator moderates, as in decides if

the content is appropriate for these articles and chooses when to publish them. The Contributor gets access to more information in that they can view all the published posts as they appear on the website and can create posts of their own. As shown in Figure 3.15 their posts can only be submitted for review.

Fig. 3.16 Press may be useful for some contributors.

Contributors also get access to a tool called **Press This** where a snippet from another website can be added to a Post. The quickest way to see how this works is to use the **Direct Link** that opens in a web page. The URL has to be as shown in Figure 3.16 and if the URL shown is used then a neat summary of what BBC News is about is formatted as a new post.

Author

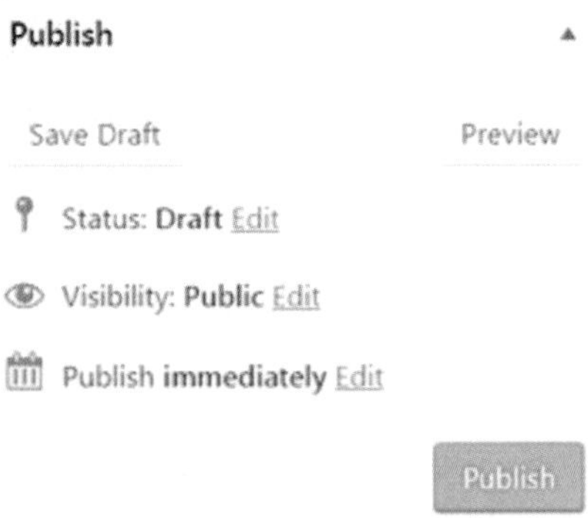

Publish

Save Draft   Preview

📍 Status: **Draft** Edit

👁 Visibility: **Public** Edit

🗓 Publish **immediately** Edit

[Publish]

Fig. 3.17 An Author is trusted with adding material to your website.

Moving up the hierarchy of roles, an **Author** can create, manage and publish their own posts. The dashboard they see when they login is almost identical to that of the **Contributor** but now there is a Publish button instead of **Submit for Review** (Refer to Figure 3.15) as shown in Figure 3.17.

Only assign this role to people who know the basics of editing on a WordPress website.

Editor

As the name implies, an **Editor** can do everything that the **Author** can do but they can now view and publish posts from the Contributors and Subscribers. This is a more powerful role because an Editor can also create new categories and tags, upload new media and add new pages. The administrator might benefit from having at least one Editor to share the duties of moderating the content on the website.

Administrators

The website creator will always be an **Administrator**, the role that can do everything. In the WordPress documentation there are references to **Super Administrators** but this refers to an Administrator that oversees multiple sites, each with its own administrator. For a single site this is not of interest.

   There is a benefit in creating a second administrator account just in case the primary one encounters a problem and the website refuses to log the administrator in. Usually this is not because of hacking but more likely a database issue. To avoid this type of problem create a second administrator now and put the details in a secure place.

More Roles

User Role Editor

User Role Editor WordPress plugin makes user roles and capabilities changing easy. Edit/add/delete WordPress user roles and capabilities.

By Vladimir Garagulya

Fig. 3.18 The User Role Editor lets an administrator make adjustments to standard WordPress roles.

If the administrator wants to refine the built-in roles there are two additional modules or plugins that might help. The User Role Editor (Figure 3.18) is a very powerful tool but one that should be used by an experienced administrator. There is also the WP Front Role that is less functional than the User Role Editor but might be useful in certain circumstances. There is much more on plugins in Chapter 7.

Time Settings

The time settings are well explained except for the **time zone** especially daylight saving time changes such as British Summer Time (BST). There are a lot of plugins to make this happen but they are not necessary. The trick is to select a **city** (Figure 3.19) rather than a time zone and WordPress will do the rest.

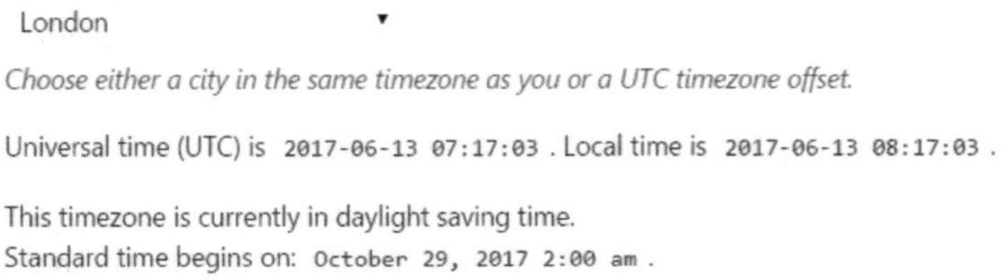

London   ▾

Choose either a city in the same timezone as you or a UTC timezone offset.

Universal time (UTC) is `2017-06-13 07:17:03` . Local time is `2017-06-13 08:17:03` .

This timezone is currently in daylight saving time.
Standard time begins on: `October 29, 2017 2:00 am` .

Fig.3.19 Make the website adjust its time automatically by starting
with a City.

For example, select London from the drop down list by scrolling upwards from the time zones and click on the  Save Changes button. If necessary, use the nearest location to your own. When the display updates WordPress has changed the time to BST and will automatically change back on the date shown. The remainder of the time section concerns the way the date and time are formatted and on which day the week starts.

Site Language

The site language defaults to US English. WordPress has some regional options including UK English. Simply select it from the drop down menu.

Things to do now

Membership   ☐ Anyone can register

Fig. 3.20 Remember to untick this box and save the change even if you don't do anything else.

Before moving on from this section make the website secure by not allowing potential users to join.   Untick the **Anyone can register** box for now to prevent spam messages (Figure 3.20).

Finally , scan all the settings for any obvious errors and click **Save Changes** before moving on to the next part of the settings.

Settings - Writing

These settings cover both adding posts or comments on posts directly on the website and also sending contributions via e-mail.

Default Post Category

If the plan is to allow visitors to add comments then they will be assigned this category tag. The drop down list will contain all the categories known to this WordPress website. If the website has just been set up then the only category available is probably **Uncategorized.** That is fine for now.

Default Post Format

There are ten formats available to use and everything will work just fine by leaving this setting as **Standard**. This is a little confusing as this means that no formatting is used but it is not a problem.

For the record the other formats are listed below but they can only be implemented by adding code to the theme. Some themes add background images and other graphics to the post or page but for a simple-to-manage website stick with the Standard format. The other formats are tempting to use but they will probably give you a lot of niggly problems.

Other Formats

aside - Typically styled without a title. Similar to a Facebook note update.

gallery - A gallery of images. Post will likely contain a gallery shortcode and will have image attachments.

link - A link to another site. Themes may wish to use the first <a href=""> tag in the post content as the external link for that post. An alternative approach could be if the post consists only of a URL, then that will be the URL and the title (post_title) will be the name attached to the anchor for it.

image - A single image. The first <img /> tag in the post could be considered the image. Alternatively, if the post consists only of a URL, that will be the image URL and the title of the post (post_title) will be the title attribute for the image.

quote - A quotation. Probably will contain a blockquote holding the quote content. Alternatively, the quote may be just the content, with the source/author being the title.

status - A short status update, similar to a Twitter status update.

video - A single video or video playlist. The first <video /> tag or object/embed in the post content could be considered the video. Alternatively, if the post consists only of a URL, that will be the video URL. It may also contain the video as an attachment to the post, if video support is enabled on the blog (like via a plugin).

audio - An audio file or playlist. Could be used for Podcasting.

chat - A chat transcript.

Posting via e-mail

This feature should be restricted to a few trusted people. It is less important now because so many people have smartphones and tablets. WordPress plan to remove this feature in a future release but it is still available in version 4.8.

Setting this up requires a good deal of knowledge of the web hosting package and is best avoided. Leave the settings as suggested by WordPress as the mail server does not exist and WordPress won't do anything.

Update Service

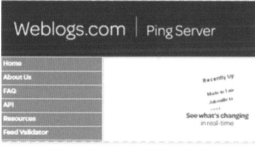

WordPress supports update services that lets your subscribers know when a blog has been updated. A very popular service is Ping-o-Matic and WordPress makes this easy to set up by listing Ping-O-Matic's server

Fig. 3.21 Another part of WordPress that you can leave using its defaults settings.

(rpc.pingomatic.com) by default (Figure 3.21).

Ping-O-Matic is a gateway site that will let other services know that there is a new entry. Weblogs is a data aggregator that lists minute by minute those blogs that have been updated. The entry can be left as is in the WordPress dashboard or deleted as it is very unlikely to cause a problem in either case.

Settings—Reading

Here is a very important setting that also appears in the theme customisation tab that sets the primary look and feel of the website.

The default option is a blog for **Your latest posts** (Figure 3.22) or have a static (front) page as the entry point to other static pages. The website can have both posts, on a page of their own, and pages and seamless access to both types is possible via menus and links.

Your Latest Posts (Blogging Site)

By default posts are added to the home page of the website. There is scope for confusion with the terms home and front pages especially if the page names have been changed at some point.

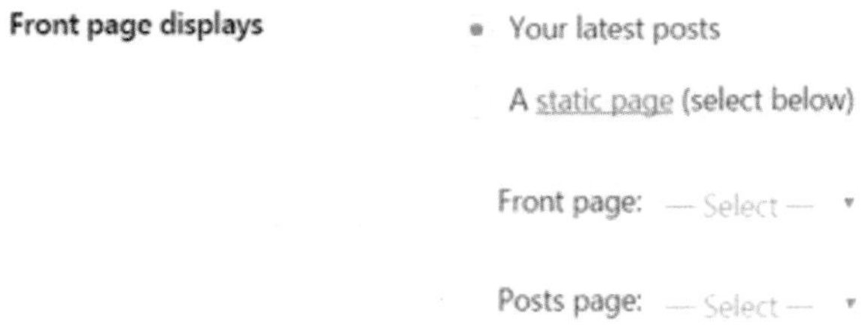

Front page displays   • Your latest posts

                                    A static page (select below)

                                    Front page: — Select — ▾

                                    Posts page: — Select — ▾

Fig. 3.22 WordPress starts with a blogging website as users are more likely to use it for that purpose.

For the setup shown in Fig 3.22 your posts will be found, for example, at **http://www.mywebsite.co.uk/wp/index.php** and not on any other pages added to the website.

In this configuration the blogging page is the page returned by the **index.php** program.

The next setting down the list, **Blog pages show at most,** sets the number of posts to display at any one time. See Figure 3.23 on the next page. Adjust this number to make the page look better in the browsers.

The **syndication feeds show the most recent** setting is not that important unless operating a very busy website.

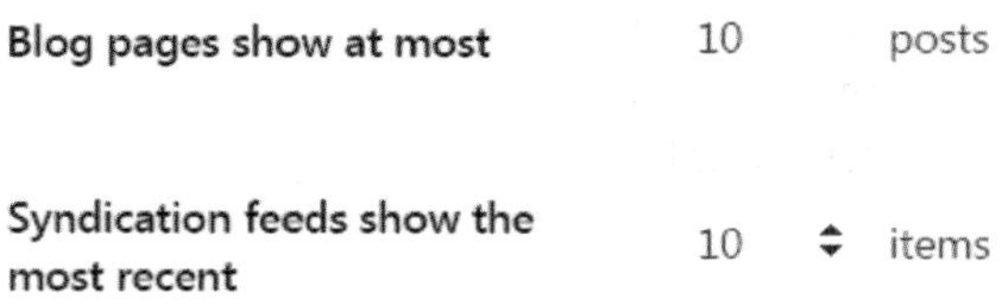

Blog pages show at most   10   posts

Syndication feeds show the most recent   10 ⬍ items

Fig. 3.23 Control your front page by limiting the number of posts at any one time.

The next option is the choice of displaying the full text or a summary from the first few lines of the article. Leave it at **Full text** as shown in Figure 3.24

Skip to the **Search Engine** section to configure the website as a blog.

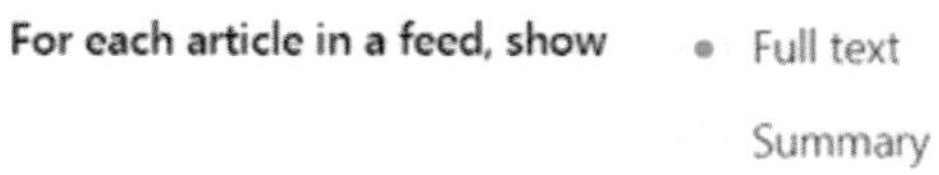

For each article in a feed, show
• Full text
  Summary

Fig. 3.24 Two display options for text.

Page Based Website

Front page displays
  Your latest posts
• A static page (select below)
  Front page: Home   ▾
  Posts page: Blogging Page ▾

Fig. 3.25 The setting to set up a page-based website.

By ticking the **static page** option (Figure 3.25) the previously greyed out dropdown menus are made available to choose a new home page that doesn't automatically change and a new page for the blogging content that updates as each new post is added.

By saving this change the posts that were previously accessed via index.php get moved to a new location typically found at **http://www.mywebsite.co.uk/wp/blogging-page** and **http://www.mywebsite.co.uk/wp/index.php** will point to **http://www.mywebsite.co.uk/wp/home/** the home page of a page-based website. The URLs are included here as a way for you to check that the internal configuration is correct.

The URLs shown above have been made simpler by WordPress for humans to understand. The 'real' URL is of this form:

http://www.mywebsite.co.uk/wp/index.php?page-id=2

I have included this long form of the URL for reference as it sometimes flashes up in the browser's address bar.

Search Engine Visibility

Search Engine Visibility   ☑ Discourage search engines from indexing this site

It is up to search engines to honor this request.

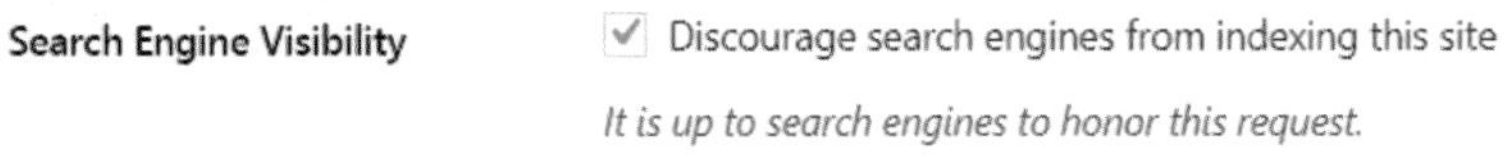

Fig. 3.26 Search engines will honour your request not to add the web pages to their index.

Google and Bing find new websites automatically and in a process called crawling will gather data for their search tools. There is a code of practice controlled by a file stored on the website named **robots.txt** or in the head part of the website's HTML coding to tell the search engines' spiders or robots to ignore some or all of the content.

Ticking the **Search Engine Visibility** box (Figure 3.26) adds a line of HTML code just below the <title> HTML tag telling the robots not to index this website but that they can still follow links found on pages . Unticking the box removes the tag and Google, Bing, Yahoo, etc. will crawl your website for pages to add to their indexes.

Sometimes it is advisable to wait until all the pages are set up, links tested, etc. but in most cases Google and Bing can handle websites under development.

Now save your configuration of either a blogging website or a page based website by clicking on **Save Changes**. Once again, remember that these options can be changed as and when required.

Settings - Discussion

Don't Allow Comments

This is one of the biggest section in settings. If the website is for information only and you do not want anyone to comment on the content then only one of these settings apply.

Open the **Dashboard -> Settings -> Default article settings** and untick the *Allow people to post comments* as shown in figure 3.27.

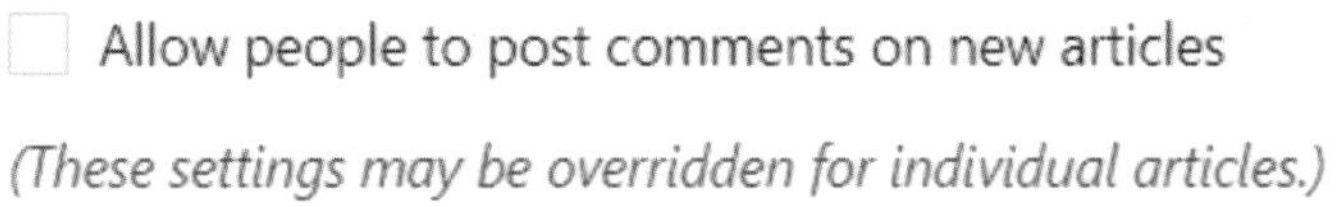

Allow people to post comments on new articles

(These settings may be overridden for individual articles.)

Fig. 3.27 Unticking this one box stops visitors to your website posting comments.

Note that this setting applies to **future posts** and that visitors can still comment on **existing posts** until the setting is changed on each one of those posts. Note also that WordPress uses the word **article** to cover both **pages** and **posts** as both can have comments made on their content. Note the comment below the option that visitors can comment on a particular post. If there is something on the website where, for example, members' comments on a proposed date for the AGM would be useful, then the next section covers how to allow comments on that single post or page.

Allow Comments on selected posts

You can apply these instructions to existing posts to disallow any future comments or to new posts that need comments while continuing to prevent comments on all other articles.

The path is **Dashboard -> Posts ->All Posts** to display a list of all the posts. To make sure that the comments are visible check the settings in the Screen Options via the drop-down menu in the top right-hand corner

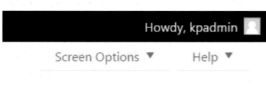

Fig. 3.28 The Screen Options menu controls how much information is displayed on each article.

as shown in Figure 3.28. Expand the drop-down menu and make sure the Comments box is ticked as shown in Figure 3.29.

Columns

☑ Author   ☑ Categories   ☑ Tags   ☑ Comments   ☑ Date

Pagination

Number of items per page: 20

View Mode

● List View   ○ Excerpt View

Fig. 3.29 Some of the screen options for the list of posts. Tick the ones that provide you with useful information. The View Mode should be set to List View.

Now scan down the list and the posts that actually have comments attached to them are listed as shown in Figure 3.30.

Date

Published
2017/03/21

Published
2016/12/06

Fig. 3.30 The Posts with comments are flagged with numbers in comments symbols.

Select the post to change by clicking on it and a new screen opens up with a lot more information on that particular post.

At the top right-hand side there are more screen options that do different things to the ones on the **post listing** screen. Ensure that the Discussion box is ticked (Figure 3.31) to see whether Comments are allowed and the Comments box is ticked to view the comments .

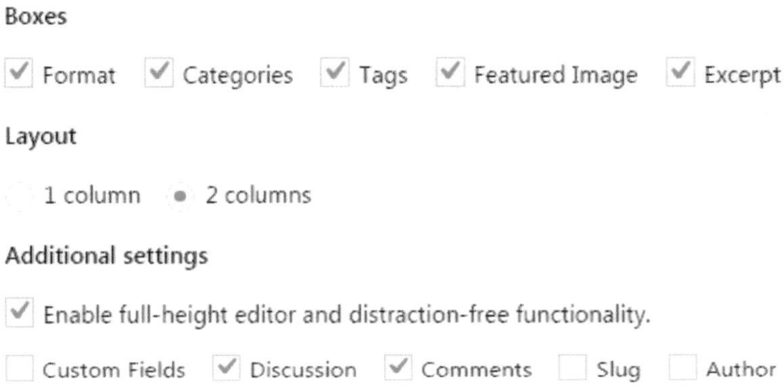

Boxes

✔ Format   ✔ Categories   ✔ Tags   ✔ Featured Image   ✔ Excerpt

Layout

○ 1 column   • 2 columns

Additional settings

✔ Enable full-height editor and distraction-free functionality.

☐ Custom Fields   ✔ Discussion   ✔ Comments   ☐ Slug   ☐ Author

Fig. 3.31 The individual posts have their own set of screen options.

Next scroll down until you see the Discussion section (Figure 3.32) and tick or untick the *Allow comments* box as required.

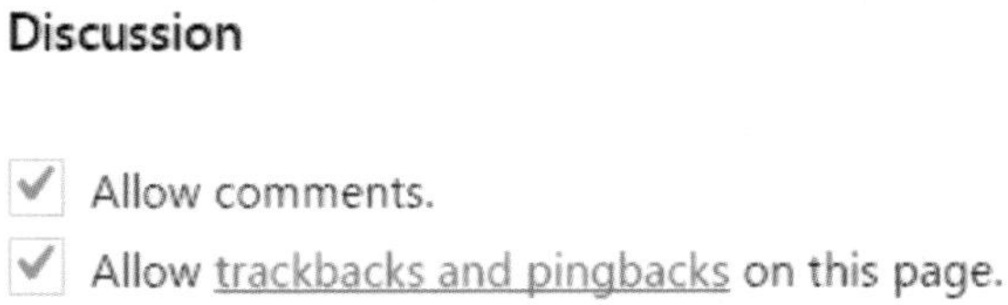

Discussion

✔ Allow comments.

✔ Allow trackbacks and pingbacks on this page.

Fig. 3.32 Control comments on individual posts by ticking or unticking the box.

Notice that as the administrator you can also add a comment possibly to let users know that the status of this post has changed , you want to reply to or correct the post and so on.

You can also use this section to disallow comments on posts that were created prior to you changing the setting.

Change Comments on Selected Pages

The equivalent path for pages is **Dashboard -> Posts ->All Pages.** Update the top level screen options (Figure 3.33) by expanding the menu on the top right of the screen and ticking the relevant boxes. Then click on Apply.

Check the list is displaying the comments icon, as it was for posts in Figure 3.29, and select the item that needs changing by clicking on it.

Again, expand the **Screen Options** section at the top of screen and once again make sure that the Discussion box is ticked (Figure 3.34).

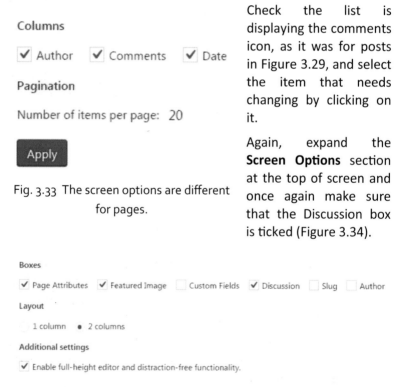

Fig. 3.33 The screen options are different for pages.

Fig. 3.34 Tick the option for Discussion to see if the page is open for comments.

Close the Screen Options to save your new settings. Scroll down the screen to allow or disallow comments. Note that to add a comment of your own the **Discussion** option will have to be changed to allow comments and the page published. Add the comment, update the page, change the comment status to disallow and update again. It is a bit long-winded but it works.

Allow Comments on Articles

Remember that these settings apply to both pages and posts. It is possible to allow comments on posts but not on pages. The converse is also possible. To do this allow people to post comments and edit the individual pages or posts to stop people adding comments to them.

Open the **Dashboard -> Settings -> Discussion** section.

Step 1   First of all, allow people to add comments to all posts and pages on your website. In the **Default article settings** tick the box to **Allow people to post comments on new articles**.

☑ Allow people to post comments on new articles

(These settings may be overridden for individual articles.)

Fig. 3.35 The comments tick box set to all posting of feedback.

Tip: I normally like to check that a setting has taken effect but if you do this while logged in to the administration section then you might get confusing results because of the high level of permissions that goes with the administrator role.

I usually test what I have done on another device but if you don't have one create another user, log out of admin and browse the website as a 'normal' user.

Step 2   In this age of malicious commenting is it good practice to put a little security in place. WordPress has two levels of security that you can use. The first is where people have to fill in a name and e-mail address but, of course, there is no real way to validate either of them (Figure 3.36). Nevertheless it can be a deterrent to at least reduce the level of what is another form of spam. WordPress can also force people to register and logged in to post comments as shown in Figure 3.37.

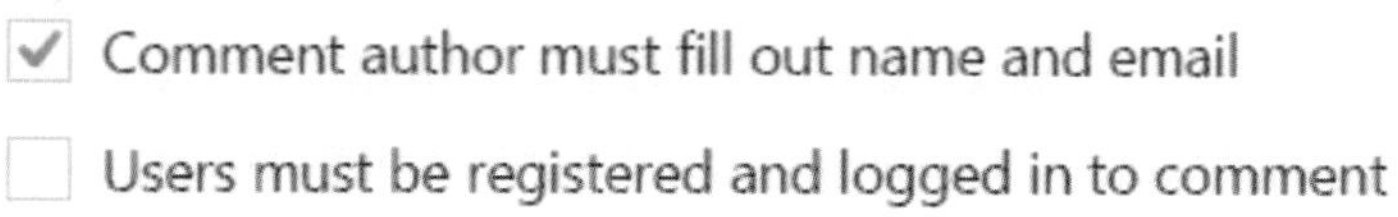

☑ Comment author must fill out name and email

☐ Users must be registered and logged in to comment

Fig. 3.36 Level one security asking for basic information.

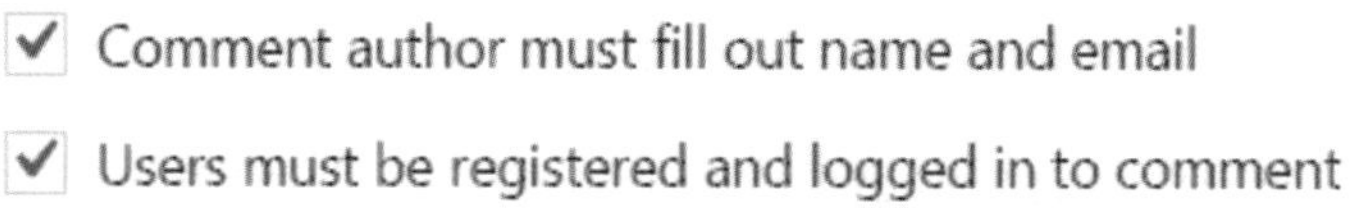

☑ Comment author must fill out name and email

☑ Users must be registered and logged in to comment

Fig. 3.37 Level Two security added.

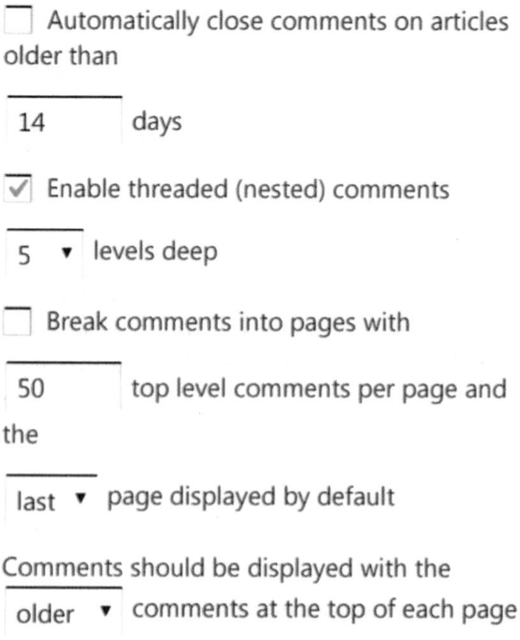

☐ Automatically close comments on articles older than

| 14 | days

☑ Enable threaded (nested) comments

| 5 ▾ | levels deep

☐ Break comments into pages with

| 50 | top level comments per page and the

| last ▾ | page displayed by default

Comments should be displayed with the
| older ▾ | comments at the top of each page

Fig. 3.38 The other options in the Discussion settings are fairly clear. You will come back to these on occasions to get your website just right.

The remainder of the other comment settings is devoted to the quantity of comments to be kept (Figure 3.38). Most of them are self explanatory and the default settings can be left unchanged.

Nested or threaded comments probably need a few words of explanation. These are comments on comments and it is always a good idea to limit this to prevent online exchanges between people with strong opinions. Alternatively, edit that particular post or page to curtail the discussion.

Email me whenever

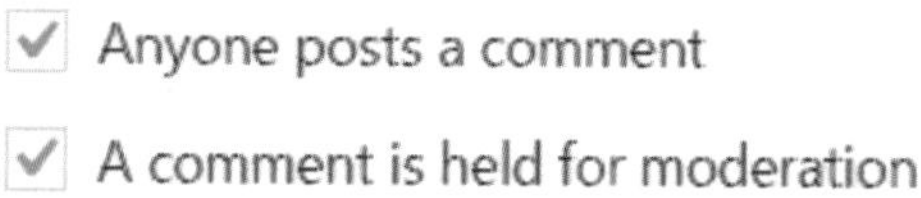

☑ Anyone posts a comment

☑ A comment is held for moderation

Fig. 3.39 Email options for the administrator.

The options selected will probably depend on how busy the website is. If it is very active then processing a lot of e-mails every day can be a chore. Before deciding, check the other settings below as a combination of them may make life a bit easier.

Before a comment appears

It may reduce the workload by letting the people who make a sensible contribution to post comments without any further intervention. Use this setting in conjunction with the settings shown in Figure 3.36 and Figure 3.37.

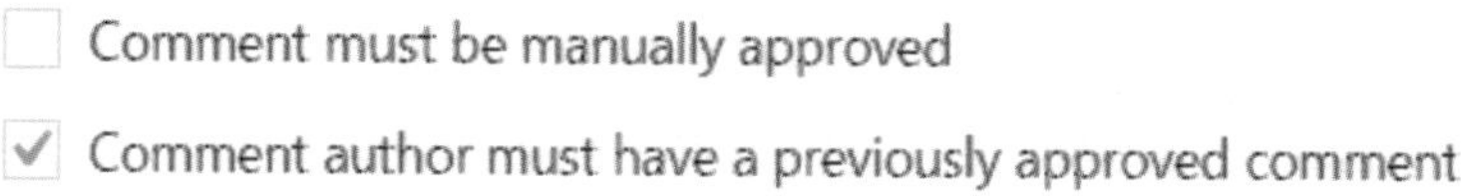

☐ Comment must be manually approved

☑ Comment author must have a previously approved comment

Fig. 3.40 Other options on comments.

Comment Moderation

Hold a comment in the queue if it contains

| 2 | or more links. (A common

characteristic of comment spam is a large number of hyperlinks.)

When a comment contains any of these words in its content, name, URL, email, or IP, it will be held in the moderation queue. One word or IP per line. It will match inside words, so "press" will match "WordPress".

Fig. 3.41 The start of the moderation options.

The first part of this section is pretty clear and I recommend that you just leave the default option as it is unless of course the website has a lot of people sending in links.

If that is likely, then you should consider upping this number to 3 or 4. Reduce it to 1 if you do not want any comment with a link added to the queue.

The second section may be useful if there is a persistent user making unhelpful, rude or provocative comments or there is a need to clean up comments. There can be other considerations of taste and decency that might influence the decision. Think carefully before putting a lot of filtering in here as it might just upset some genuine users.

There are a few examples in Figure 3.42 of what you could put in the box once the information is gathered together. As you can see a website, some words, a user by name, a user identified by an e-mail address and a four digit number (IP address) have been added to the filter. In the moderation queue for a page or a post there will be some additional information about who posted the comment.

When a comment contains any of these words in its content, name, URL, email, or IP, it will be held in the moderation queue. One word or IP per line. It will match inside words, so "press" will match "WordPress".

```
www.spamspam.co.uk
porn
vile
fred bloggs
fred@bademail.com
123.189.213.86
```

Fig. 3.42 Examples of the filtering that can be applied to stop spammers in their tracks.

Date

Published
2017/03/21

Fig. 3.43 Comments are available for this post.

On the side panel menu on the dashboard click on **Post —> All Posts** to get a listing. Near the right edge look for the comment icons with coloured numbers. Then click on the symbol (see Figure 3.43) to open the full list of comments , they are only for that post and not a global list, held in the queue for moderation

The first column in the moderation queue provides information of who make the comment. Be careful using the IP address (88.111.132.230) (Figure 3.44) as this may be an IP shared by several users in a geographical area. The e-mail address is a good place to start but before adding a user's name do try to make it as unique as possible. Also note

kevin
kpryan01@tiscali.co.uk
88.111.132.230

that the filtering process will match parts of words so *evil* and *devil* will be blocked if the filter word is *bedevilled* . A URL is a safer way to block such content.

Fig. 3.44 Technical information on a user.

Comment Blacklist

This section is the same as the Comment Moderation control but differs in that comments that satisfy any of the criteria specified will be consigned to spam rather than a moderation list.

Don't worry if a genuine comment ends up in the spam list as it can be found and restored very quickly.

Open the **Comments** tab on the dashboard , select **Spam** to open the list of items (Figure 3.45) and then take action to restore the item.

All (8) | Pending (3) | Approved (5) | Spam (0) | Trash (0)

Bulk Actions   ▾   Apply   All comment types ▾

Fig. 3.45 Look in the Trash for any comments.

Select the item or items by ticking the box next to it and from the **Bulk Actions** choose **Not Spam** and the comment will be linked to the Post or Page.

Restore   ▾   Apply

☐   Author

☐   kevin
      kpryan01@tiscali.co.uk
  88.111.132.230

3.46 The item that went into the trash by mistake being restored.

Hovering over the item will also give you a **Not Spam** option along with an option to **Delete Permanently** .

Trash may also have comments that need to be restored, deleted or sent to the Spam list. Comments usually end up in the trash due to human error.

Avatars

An avatar is an image in the form of a little picture that represents a real person online. The easiest option is not to show avatars at all by leaving the box unticked.

Avatar Display   Show Avatars

Fig. 3.47 The easiest option is not to have avatars. Your website will work perfectly well without them.

Fig. 3.48 Mystery man, identicon and monstered.

If you want to know a bit more then tick the box, **Show Avatars**, that enables two more sets of options on controlling the images to prevent offensive images being used and providing a default image for those users who find it unnecessary or don't want to provide a picture of themselves.

Fig. 3.49 Wavatar, retro and blank.

Some of the default ones are OK and others have a limited appeal. Your website may warrant their use but this is something you can do at a later date.

Gravatar

A Gravatar is a **G**lobally **R**ecognized **Avatar**. The profile image is uploaded and the user profile created just once. This personal Gravatar can be used to participate in any Gravatar-enabled site, and the user's Gravatar image will automatically follow them there. Gravatar allows users to self-rate their images so that they can indicate if an image is appropriate for a certain audience.

- G — Suitable for all audiences
- PG — Possibly offensive, usually for audiences 13 and above
- R — Intended for adult audiences above 17
- X — Even more mature than above

3.50 Gravatar settings are like film ratings.

By default, only 'G' rated images are displayed unless the website administrator decides to allow higher ratings. Using the r= or rating= parameters, the administrator can specify one of the following ratings to request images up to and including that rating:

●**g**: suitable for display on all websites with any audience type.

●**pg**: may contain rude gestures, provocatively dressed individuals, the lesser swear words, or mild violence.

●**r**: may contain such things as harsh profanity, intense violence, nudity, or hard drug use.

x: may contain hardcore sexual imagery or extremely disturbing violence.

It is advisable to accept the default settings supplied by WordPress and only have avatars or profile pictures suitable for everyone.

Settings - Media

Here you can control the size of the various images, thumbnail, medium and large, on your website. Chances are you won't have to change the defaults.

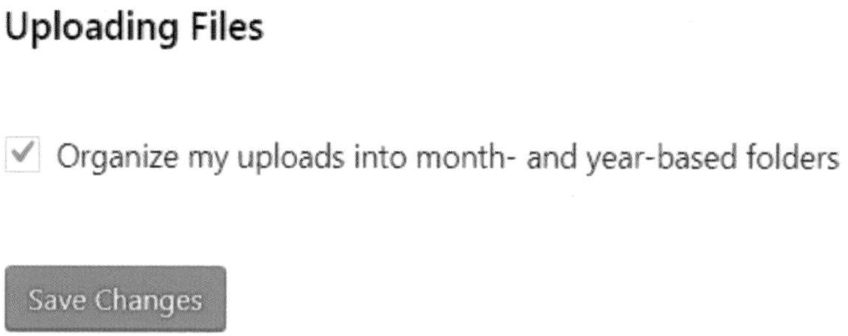

Uploading Files

✓ Organize my uploads into month- and year-based folders

Save Changes

Fig. 3.51 WordPress likes to organize its files by year and month.

The other setting (Figure 3.51) tells WordPress how to organize your image files. The options are the default , well organized or a big bucket with everything in it.

Permalinks

The Permalinks settings tab allows you to choose a number of structures for the various objects, such as posts, pages and images, stored in WordPress. The choice is yours but my two favourites are the default option of Day and Name or Post Name. To be honest, it doesn't really matter that much which one you choose. Leave it at the default and just see if your website users have any thoughts on the matter.

You have now completed the Settings section of your website and you are now ready to start learning how to create content. Adding content may require you to come back to the settings to adjust a few things.

4

WordPress Editor

WordPress comes with a default editor and usually there is no reason to change this. Other editors are available but they may not be updated as regularly as the built-in one. The editor is a modified version of the well-known TinyMCE software used in many other packages.

One of the essential features an editor must have is **copy and paste from Microsoft Word** and this feature, although not very obvious , is built in. There is no button on the toolbar as is sometimes found in versions of this product. The same editor is used for posts and pages and in some plugins.

The TinyMCE editor is a plugin but does not appear in the plugin list to prevent it being accidently deleted. Another text editor can be downloaded and once **activated** will replace TinyMCE. To change back simply **de-activate** it and the default editor will be re-enabled.

Opening the Editor

Fig. 4.1 Add New opens the editor.

There are a number of ways to access the editor . Clicking on either **Posts** or **Pages** in the dashboard displays a list of posts or pages and at the top of the screen is a button to add a new article that automatically opens the editor. Clicking on one of the posts or pages will also open the editor. Hovering over a post or page in the top-level list reveals the **Edit** and a **Quick Edit** option. The latter is used to control how the item is treated by WordPress and does not display the content.

The Editing Screen - Part 1

The page or post screen has a number of sections and it is important to get familiar with them first of all by exploring them in blocks of functions. Figure 4.2 shows a screenshot of the single **Edit Page** screen broken into seven numbered sections.

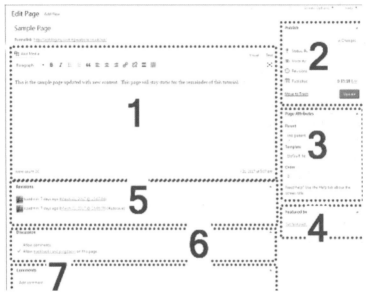

Fig. 4.2 The top half of a typical post or page. Section 1 is the editing pane.

Section 1 (Applies to Posts and Pages)

The editing pane covers most of the screen area and is where the content of a post or page is added or changed. There are three modes controlled by the buttons on the right-hand side of the toolbar area.

Visual— displays the content in WYSIWYG (what you see is what you get) mode and is the mode used most of the time.

Text — removes the toolbar and displays the text and any HTML

Visual   Text

Fig. 4.3 The editor's
three modes.

tags included in the content. This mode is useful if there is a need to work directly with HTML. HTML (**H**yperText **M**arkup **L**anguage) is a library of tags, enclosed between brackets <> that tells the browser how to format the content.

Distraction Free—the four pointed symbol under these options toggle between the full featured screen with seven panels and the distraction free one that just leaves the editing pane.

Toolbar

Add Media

Paragraph   ▾   **B**   *I*   ☰   ☰   "   ☰   ☰   ☰   🔗   ⚏   ☰   ⌨

Fig. 4.4 The editor toolbar in its simplest mode.

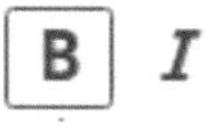

B   *I*   Some of this toolbar is familiar and the buttons to change text to Bold or Italics probably need no explanation.

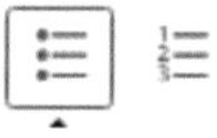

☰   ☰   The next two insert a Bulleted or Numbered list.

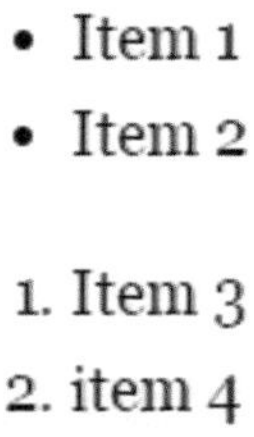

- Item 1
- Item 2

1. Item 3
2. item 4

The formatting is useful in presenting information in a clear way. These are toggle switches that stay active until they are disabled.

Blockquotes

This is often quite a confusing aspect of the TinyMCE editor. The concept behind it is that clicking this button will add a similar symbol into the text to show that the section of text is a direct quote by somebody. The problem is that the button may not do anything and this is often because the theme does not support it.

As a test enter some text and then click or tap the blockquote button and probably the text may shift to the right or change in some other way.

Next click the Text button and notice that the text is now topped and tailed with some HTML tags as shown in Figure 4.5.

This website is changing rapidly

during June as new material is added.
<blockquote>Check back for another

update on the 19th.</blockquote>

Fig. 4.5 The blockquote button adds HTML to the text.

On the website and in the visual editor the line of text between the <blockquote> tags is now in a different font.

The page on the website is shown in Figure 4.6 , with the carriage returns removed, but does not have a graphical quotation mark.

This website is changing rapidly during June as new material is added.

Check back for another update on the 19th.

Fig. 4.6 The lower line of text has changed to a new font but is still missing the expected quotation marks.

If the Blockquotes feature is important to your particular style of website it can be added into the theme but it is really a task for a website developer as it requires a knowledge of another web technology called CSS, short for Cascading Style Sheets.

In summary, this is a feature of the editor that is best to ignore. You now know what it does and how it can be a distraction.

Text Justification

 Like Microsoft Word and other text editors TinyMCE has options to justify or align the text to either the left margin, in the middle of the text area or to the right margin.

Links

 Links are useful to reference resources internally on your website or to point visitors to interesting material on another website. A nice feature in WordPress is that both pages and posts can be linked to.

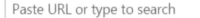

Fig. 4.7 Clicking or tapping the link button opens an input box.

Clicking on the button opens a box (Figure 4.7) that assumes you want to link to a URL or search for content on the internal website.

The search checks the title of the posts and pages looking for a word match. Assuming there are a few articles on the website type in a word from one of the title , as shown in the example in Figure 4.8.

Fig. 4.8 The search box responds to the word typed into it.

The search word is *second,* and a post with that name is returned in the search results. If that is correct click the Apply button to insert it into the post being edited. However there are still a few

http://second
second

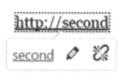

things to do to create a properly formatted link and WordPress changes the screen to another option panel. Clicking on the pencil simply exits back to the previous screen but at least it is now clear that WordPress has not created a properly formatted URL. It looks like it might link to the internal page but it doesn't link to anything internally or externally.

http://second
http://second
Link options

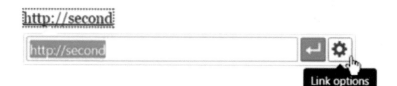

Fig. 4.9 The first pass at creating a link has resulted in a mis-formed URL that is a dead end.

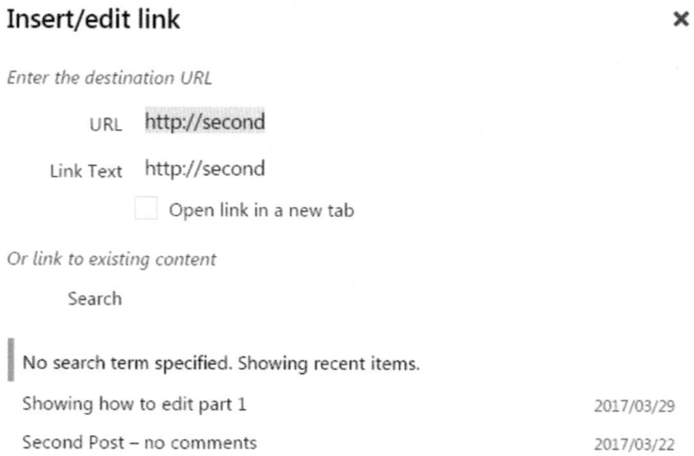

Insert/edit link
Enter the destination URL
URL http://second
Link Text http://second
Open link in a new tab
Or link to existing content
Search
No search term specified. Showing recent items.
Showing how to edit part 1 2017/03/29
Second Post – no comments 2017/03/22

Fig. 4.10 This pane is much clearer and easier to work with.

To double check use the editor's text mode and look for a line of text similar to a permalink. Sometimes, WordPress seems to have properly formatted the link but it has failed to insert the correct HTML code into the page or post.

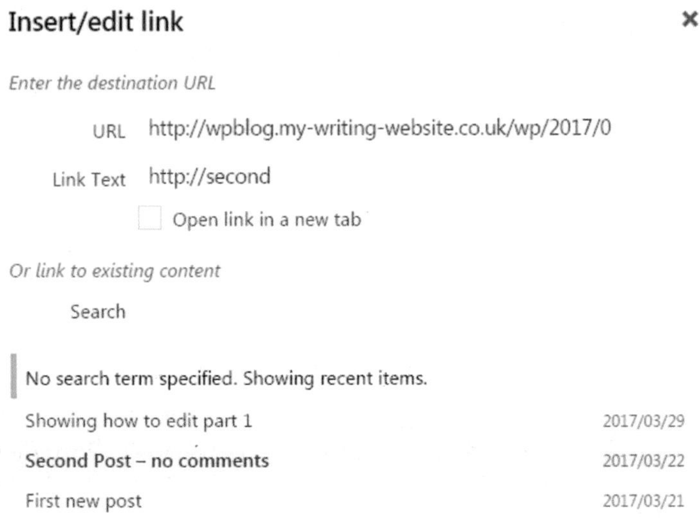

Insert/edit link   ✕

Enter the destination URL

URL   http://wpblog.my-writing-website.co.uk/wp/2017/0

Link Text   http://second

⬜ Open link in a new tab

Or link to existing content

Search

▎No search term specified. Showing recent items.

Showing how to edit part 1   2017/03/29

Second Post – no comments   2017/03/22

First new post   2017/03/21

Fig. 4.11 Note that the URL field now has a fully formed link in it
and it linking to the internal post highlighted in darker grey.

The next step in putting this right is to click on the **gear wheel** (Figure 4.9) type icon and start editing the link options. Here are many more options and notice that the URL is not long enough and that the link text is not user friendly.

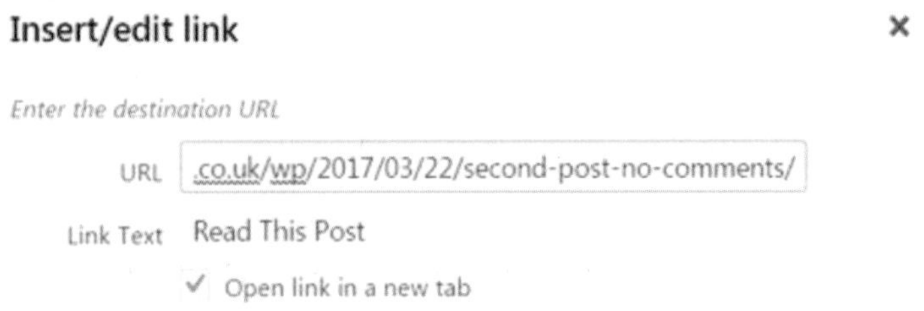

Insert/edit link   ✕

Enter the destination URL

URL   .co.uk/wp/2017/03/22/second-post-no-comments/

Link Text   Read This Post

✓ Open link in a new tab

Fig. 4.12 The Link Text has been changed to a sensible phrase.

At the bottom of this window is a scrollable list of all the posts and pages. The post to include in the new article is listed and clicking on that post to highlight updates the URL to correctly access that post.

Next change the link text to be more meaningful (Figure 4.12) to a visitor to the website, then scroll along the URL box (Figure 4.13) to the end of that line of text to check that there is a fully

Read This Post

wpblog.my-writing-website.co.uk/.../second-post-no-comments

Fig. 4.13 Check the end of the URL string to make sure it is valid.

formatted URL there and the box is ticked to open a new web page so when someone opens this article in either another tab or instance of the browser they can quickly go back to the original page. Depending on your browser setup this setting will normally open a new tab.

Back on the new post, in the editor, the effects of the changes are now visible usually through a change in the colour of the text to show that it is a link and highlighting the text shows the URL. Type a space and it will disappear.

Finally here is how to check that everything is OK. Click the Text button next to the Visual one and there should be HTML formatted code like this:

<a href="http://wpblog.my-writing-website.co.uk/
wp/2017/03/22/second-post-no-comments/"
target="_blank">Read This Post</a>

There is no need to know much about HTML to understand what this means as after the *href* tag is the URL and before the final <a> is the link text.

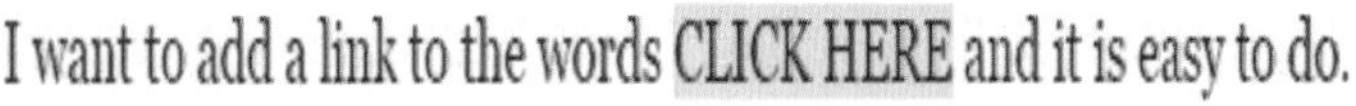

I want to add a link to the words **CLICK HERE** and it is easy to do.

Fig. 4.14 Highlight any words in a sentence and click on
the link button to create a hyper-link.

Adding a Link to Text

This is easy to do by highlighting the words already in the
article that are to form the link text. Then click on the inset
link button and follow the instructions above to fix any issues.

Removing a Link in Text

To remove a link highlight the link text and click this button.
The text is not removed or changed.

Read More

- - - - - - - - - - - - - - - - MORE -

Fig. 4.15 The Read More visual indicator in text.

This tag causes a lot of problems as it is theme dependent
and sometimes WordPress fails to insert an excerpt followed
by the invitation to Read More. Click on the button and the editor
will probably insert a line of text like this (Figure 4.15). This is a
good sign that your theme might support this feature. Place the
cursor after the end of the dotted line, type Return and enter
some text. Then Update the post or page to Publish it. If the
theme supports this feature then a Continue Reading link appears
on the website.

Emoticons

The editor has a number of emoticons , coloured faces
showing emotions, to include in articles and comments.

Extending the Editor

The final icon on the toolbar is a toggle key that gives you a slightly extended set of options.

    As the graphic suggests this is the strikethrough function.

—   This adds the HTML code to insert a horizontal line into a post or page.

A ▼   Here you can select the colour of the text with a handy colour chart.

⊘   The eraser icon is to clear formatting.

    This is to paste something from the clipboard as text rather than carrying over the format of the document from where the text came from.

⋮⋮   This pair of buttons increase or decrease indents by inserting tabs into the text.

↰ ↱   These are the undo and redo buttons that function on the article being edited. The audit trail is lost when the editor is closed.

❓   A help button that lists the keyboard shortcuts for many tasks in TinyMCE, for those rare occasions when the graphical interface has problems. There is a list of the most useful shortcuts on page 162.

The symbol button opens up a list of currency symbols, mathematical functions, the Greek alphabet and the most common accented characters.

Post or Page Formatting

The final area of the TinyMCE Word Processor is the general

Paragraph	(Shift+Alt+7)
Heading 1	(Shift+Alt+1)
Heading 2	(Shift+Alt+2)
Heading 3	(Shift+Alt+3)
Heading 4	(Shift+Alt+4)
Heading 5	(Shift+Alt+5)
Heading 6	(Shift+Alt+6)
`Preformatted`	

Paragraph ▼ formatting of the text using some pre-set HTML tags. The options are in the Paragraph drop down menu that defaults to the most useful option which is Paragraph. Opening the menu reveals seven other options showing the heading fonts available.

A common way and some would say an increasingly outdated way of adding structure to a web page is to use headings to divide the content into logical sections. The HTML specification only allows for six levels and that is more than enough. Figure 4.16 is a short piece of text using **Heading 1**, some normal text with the **Paragraph** option and then a sub-section using **Heading 2**.

Table Tennis Results

Here are the results for the first division teams.

Team A - West Division 1

Fig. 4.16 Above, part of a post with the Header 1 and Header 2 formatting applied.

Switching to the TEXT viewer shows that the information sent to a browser will look like this.

```
<h1>Table Tennis Results</h1>
Here are the results for the first division teams.
<h2>Team A - West Division 1</h2>
```

Fig. 4.17 The formatting as translated into HTML tags.

Figure 4.17 shows that Heading 1 is shown as a pair of HTML tags, <h1></h1> and Heading 2 as <h2></h2>. For Heading 1, <h1> is the start tag and </h1> is the close tag and any text after the latter will be in the default font. Each web browser interprets the heading tags slightly differently. Figure 4.16 is how Chrome has interpreted the tags and the Heading 1 text is shown in a bigger font than the Heading 2 text.

There is no need to start with Heading 1, and could use Heading 3 first and then Heading 5 but if these tags are used it is best to work downwards rather than suddenly switch to a higher Heading mid-way in your post.

One final point on Heading tags. Use the top level tag just once and then the lower ones can be used more than once.

The Preformatted Option

The final option is the preformatted one and it is best demonstrated by using the test of writing a sentence to see what happens.

```
Here is some more text
using the preformatted option
```

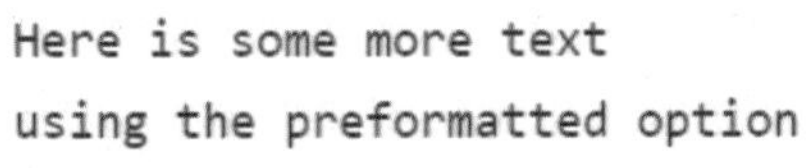

Fig. 4.18 Preformatted text.

The editor simply inserts two tags, <pre></pre>. The HTML <pre> tag is used to indicate preformatted text. Like other HTML tags the text being marked up is enclosed between a start tag <pre> and a close tag </pre>. Browsers normally render *pre* text in a fixed-pitched font, with the whitespace intact, and without word wrap. This might be useful at some point but other options such as tables offer a lot more control.

Chrome and Firefox render the code as shown in Figure 4.19 keeping any carriage returns. Other browsers may interpret it slightly differently and the output may change with browser updates

Second Post – no comments

BY   PUBLISHED MARCH 22, 2017   UPDATED SEPTEMBER 2, 2017

Table Tennis Results

Here are the results for the first division teams.

Team A – West Division 1

Fig. 4.19 This block of text has the header tags applied and then the whole block has been preformatted.

TinyMCE Advanced

Even after enabling the extended toolbar the functionality of the editor may still seem a pale shadow of what other word processors offer. Help is at hand with the aid of plugins, the best of which is TinyMCE Advanced. Do not confuse this plugin with Advanced TinyMCE Configuration.

Fig. 4.20 The fully extended toolbar in the editor.

This plugin adds the tools to include tables in the posts and pages, use new fonts and formatting and print your posts. This plugin, or additional software module, is a recommended add-on and installing this plugin is quick and easy.

The process of finding, installing and activating plugins is covered in Chapter 7 but this plugin adds so much functionality that a quick guide is included in this section. Please refer to Chapter 7 for more details if the installation has problems.

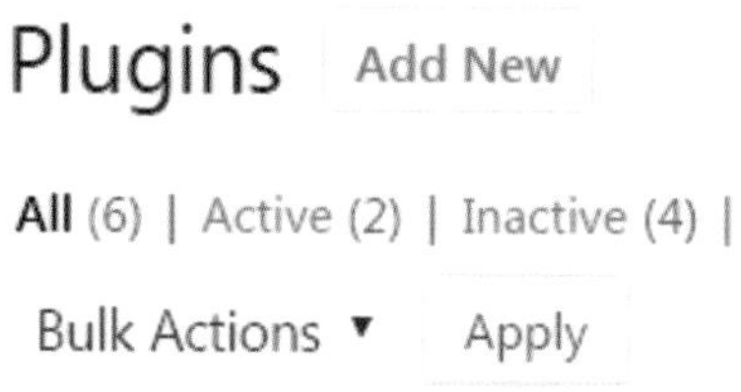

Plugins Add New

All (6) | Active (2) | Inactive (4) |

Bulk Actions ▾   Apply

Fig. 4.21 Add a new plugin.

On the dashboard menu click on Plugins and you will see a list of all installed extensions.   Click on **Add New** and search for this plugin using the search box.

Keyword ▾ TinyMCE Advanced

Fig. 4.22 Search for this plugin using the exact phrase shown above.

TinyMCE Advanced

Extends and enhances TinyMCE, the WordPress Visual Editor.

By Andrew Ozz

The results give a list of all the matches and TinyMCE Advanced is top of the list. Click on **Install Now** to add it to the plugins.

TinyMCE Advanced

Activate   Edit   Delete

Fig. 4.23 TinyMCE options in the plugins.

Next return to the dashboard, click on Plugins once more and look for the TinyMCE Advanced listing. Click on **Activate** to complete the installation process.

Go back to a post and open an item for editing. Notice anything different? The advanced editor has changed the layout of the editor as shown in Figure 4.24.

File ▾   Edit ▾   Insert ▾   View ▾   Format ▾   Table ▾   Tools ▾

Fig. 4.24 The editor has a toolbar thanks to the Advanced plugin.

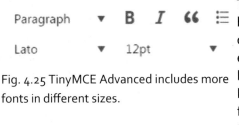

Paragraph ▼   **B** *I* **"** ≔
Lato ▼   12pt ▼

Fig. 4.25 TinyMCE Advanced includes more fonts in different sizes.

There is a new top menu bar with dropdown options and the original extended toolbar has been shuffled around a bit with more fonts and font sizes available (Figure 4.25)

All in all, the editor now looks more like the ones in the various Office packages.

TinyMCE Advanced Configuration

The plugin installs another menu item under the Settings section. Here buttons can be added to the toolbars by dragging and dropping them.

Many of the options are included in the top menu bar. There are two unused toolbars for more refinement.

Simply save the changes to update the editor. There are many options below the toolbar configuration area and the recommendation is to leave all them , apart from the option to use a more standard set of font sizes, in their default state.

Fig. 4.26 Look for the a new entry under Settings.

Section 2—Publishing (Posts and Pages)

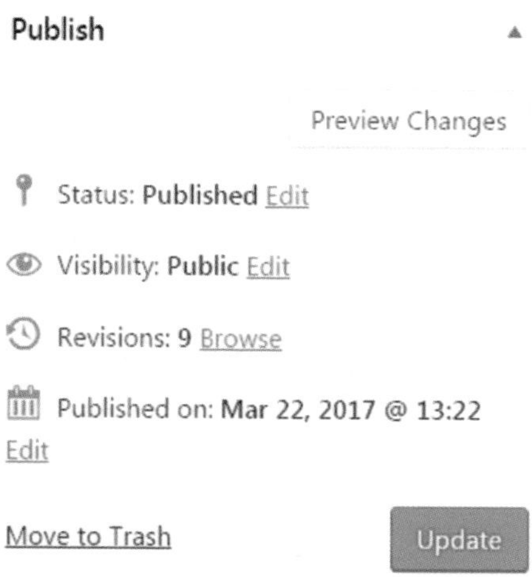

Publish

Preview Changes

Status: Published Edit

Visibility: Public Edit

Revisions: 9 Browse

Published on: Mar 22, 2017 @ 13:22
Edit

Move to Trash

Fig. 4.27 The Publish pane on the editing screen.

The publish section is straightforward. Working down from the top (Figure 4.27) the first button lets the editor **Preview** the **Changes** made to the article BEFORE anyone else sees them. To discard all the changes in one go exit out of the article and reopen it.

The next line is the current **Status** of the page or post. Clicking on the underlined Edit opens a dropdown menu listing three possible options of **Published**, **Pending Review** or **Draft**. Change the status as needed.

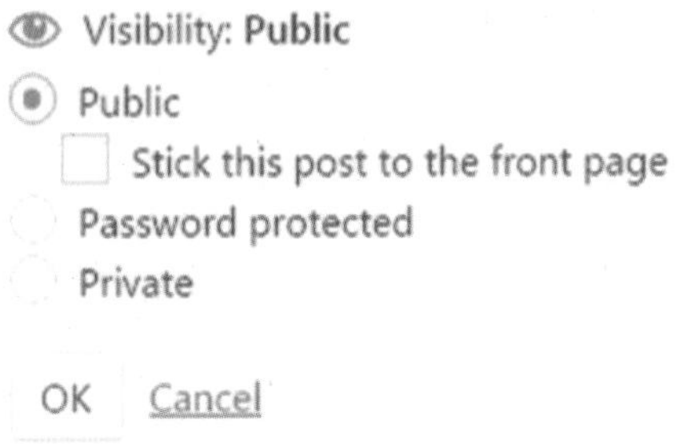

Visibility: **Public**

(•) Public

☐ Stick this post to the front page

Password protected

Private

OK   Cancel

Fig. 4.28 More publishing options.

Moving down to the next line (Fig. 4.28) starting with **Visibility** there is another Edit option. This opens a slightly different set of options that vary depending on whether the article being edited is a Post or a Page. The article can be Public and if it is a Post it can be turned into a '**Sticky**' **Post** that is always on the front page, or **Password protected** for a reason or **Private**.

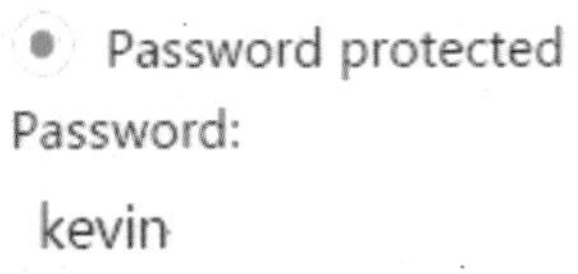

(•) Password protected

Password:

kevin

Fig. 4.29 The password can be very simple as WordPress does not enforce any rules.

Choosing to add a password opens yet another box to attach a password to this post, as shown in Figure 4.29. WordPress does not specify anything like password length or a mixture of characters and it is displayed in the clear. The post is visible to everyone but can only be opened by those with a password.

Setting the post to **Private** limits its visibility to the editors and administrators registered on the website. This can be a useful collaboration feature where articles are polished before release to the general public. The final Edit option (Fig. 4.30) in this section of the editing screen is about browsing revisions of the post or page. This can help if an important section has been deleted by accident or there is a query from the public.

Status: **Published** Edit

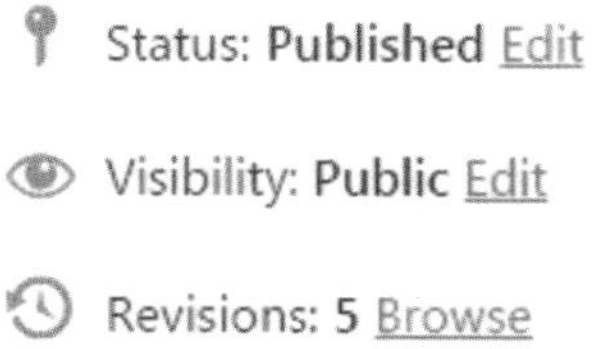

👁 Visibility: **Public** Edit

🕒 Revisions: 5 Browse

Fig. 4.30 Revisions tallies all the changes made to the page or post.

The Revisions screen has buttons to move between Previous and Next and also a slider to make scanning easier. Ticking the Compare any two revisions box adds a second button to the slider bar in case the change is a subtle one.

There is also an option to restore a complete previous revision. Once happy with the selection click on **Restore this Version** to replace the text in the post or page.

Do this a couple of times to note that WordPress logs the change as another revision rather than repositioning the articles in the revision queue.

The last thing needed is to Update the item so that it is **re-published** or deleted altogether by selecting **Move to Trash**. This is not as final as it sounds because WordPress, in common with other systems, holds onto all the trash until you decide to empty it.

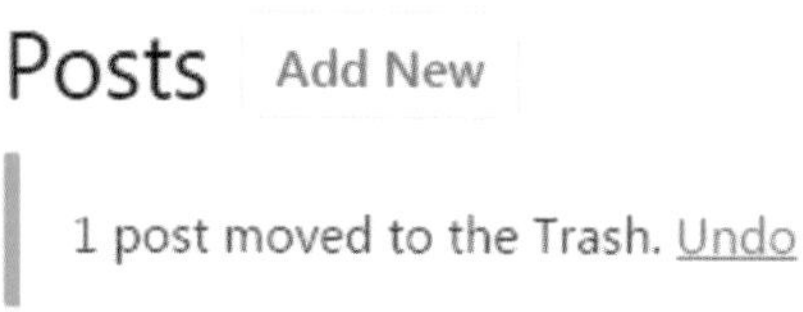

Posts   Add New

1 post moved to the Trash. Undo

4.31 You can recover a post from the trash before leaving the editing screen by clicking **Undo**.

Clicking **Move to Trash** removes the article from the published list of articles, sends the item to the Trash list and returns to either the Post or Page list to select another item.

Notice that, at the top of the screen is the option to immediately undo this. The article can still be retrieved later on although it may not be immediately obvious how to do this on the WordPress dashboard.

Recover Article from Trash

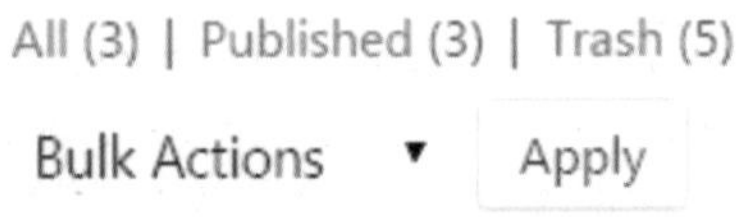

All (3) | Published (3) | Trash (5)

Bulk Actions ▼   Apply

Fig. 4.32 Summary of all the posts in WordPress.

We have touched on this earlier in the book (page 48) but it is worth reminding ourselves how the Trash function in WordPress works.

At the top of Posts or Pages listing is a summary (Figure 4.32) of all the posts or pages in the system. To get this listing select Posts (List All) or Pages (List All) from the main WordPress menu.

Clicking on the **Trash** link opens a list of all the articles in the trash list. Tick the box next to the article you want to restore and from the **Bulk Actions** drop down menu select **Restore**. Alternatively hover over the item and the same option will be highlighted underneath it. Note that there is also an option in that list to **permanently delete** selected items. The article is restored with the same status and visibility as before so it will immediately re-appear on the website.

Empty Trash

Finally, in the Trash screen there is a button to empty all the trash in one go. It is good housekeeping practice to do this periodically.

Section 3—Page Attributes (Pages Only)

Only pages have attributes. Figure 4.33 overleaf shows the three options in this section.

Parent -   Like menus you can nest pages, that is to say make a new page subordinate to another. The top level is the parent and the other levels are child pages. The default is **(no parent)** and if your website has a few pages then don't bother changing it.

Why would you want to have a nest of pages? Primarily, it is to bring order to a multi-page website by grouping similar topics

Page Attributes

Parent

(no parent)   ▼

Template

Default Template ▼

Order

0

Fig. 4.33 The page
attributes set of options.

together and show, in the URL, where one page is expanding on an idea in the parent page.

Template - In WordPress you can create a variant of your theme or template called a child theme. This is not covered in this book. Just leave the setting as **Default Template.**

Order - This allows you to change the order of the pages in the **All Pages** list. It doesn't change their order in the menus.

Section 4 - Featured Image (Pages Only)

Picking a featured image takes you to the Media Library where

Featured Image   ▲

Click the image to edit or update

Remove featured image

Fig. 4.34 Click to edit or remove it.

you can select an image already stored there or upload a new one. WordPress will add a full sized version of that image to the beginning of your page text. To reduce the size of the image click on it to edit it. This opens the media library again and on the right hand side click on Edit Image so that you can scale it in size.

In the Image Editor you can crop the image and change its orientation.

Section 5—Revisions (Pages and Posts)

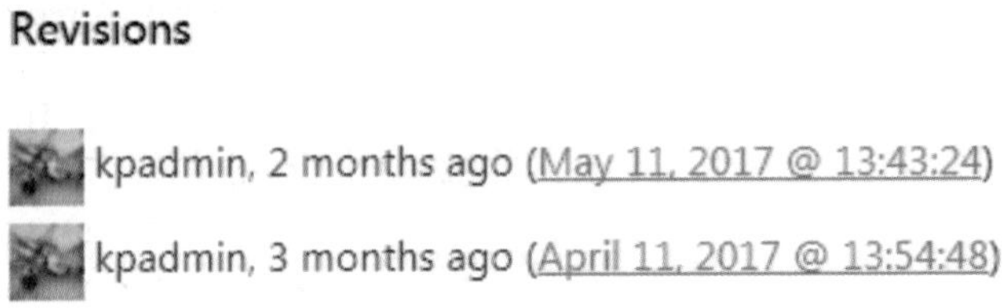

Revisions

 kpadmin, 2 months ago (May 11, 2017 @ 13:43:24)

kpadmin, 3 months ago (April 11, 2017 @ 13:54:48)

Fig. 4.35 All the revisions are listed in time order.

Selecting one of the revisions opens the revision screen (see page 67) we discussed earlier in this chapter.

Section 6— Discussions (Pages and Posts)

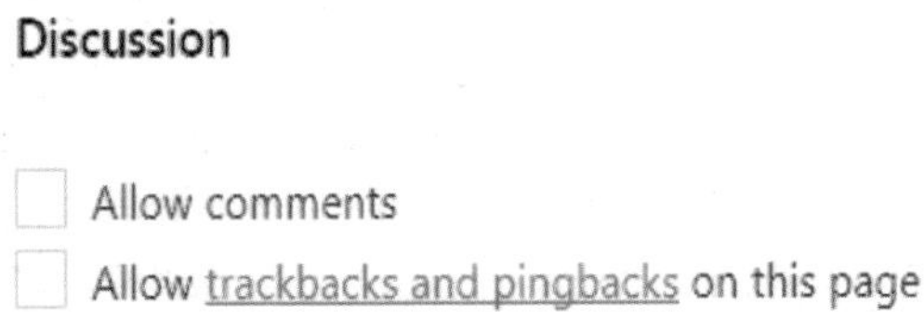

Discussion

☐ Allow comments

☐ Allow trackbacks and pingbacks on this page

Fig. 4.36 The options on discussion or comments.

Allowing or stopping comments has been covered in the Settings chapter. There is another tick box below the **Allow Comments** on trackbacks and pingbacks and this is best left unticked. Do click on the highlighted link if you want an explanation of what they are for.

Section 7— Comments

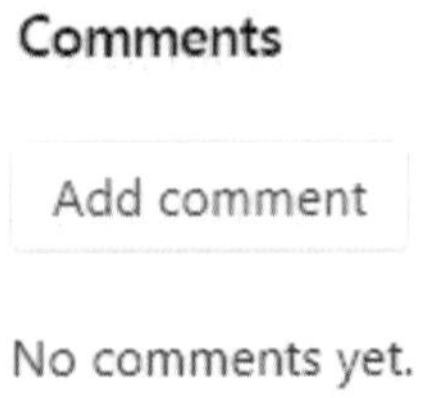

Comments

Add comment

No comments yet.

Fig. 4.37 Comments.

The comments pane has two functions. It lets the editor or administrator add comments to a page or post and also lists any comments already attached to a page or post. Figure 4.37 shows that this particular page has not attracted any comments to date.

As a test, click on the Add comment button to

see how to do this. The best way to give you an introduction to the Comments editor is by a short example. Fig 4.38 shows most of the buttons in this **text editor.** To add a comment just enter the text without any embellishments and then click on **Add Comment** that updates the post or page with a comment.

Comments

Add new Comment

b	i	link	b-quote	del	ins

ul	ol	li	code	close tags	¶

Fig. 4.38 The comments editor is a text editor working with HTML tags. The image misses out the IMG (insert image tag).

If you want to highlight any portion of the text then select either using your mouse or a swipe action and then click on either the BOLD (key with a small letter b) or Italics (small letter i) to add the HTML code.

b	i	link	b-quote	del	ins	img	ul

```
<ol>
<strong>This text in bold</strong></ol>
<ul>
<em>I want this in Italics</em></ul>
```

Fig. 4.39 Bold adds a <strong> tag and Italics an <em> tag. The others do not work as they refer to lists.

Figure 4.39 has some text with a few tags added. Figure 4.40 shows the same text in a comment.

 kpadmin ⊙ August 11, 2017 at 4:09 pm (Edit)**This text in bold**
I want this in Italics

Fig. 4.40 The two lines have picked up the highlighting entered.

The Editor Screen—Part 2

4.41 Posts have additional options to work through.

There are a few more areas to cover that are marked in Figure 4.41 as sections 8 to 11.

Section 8—Post Formatting

WordPress supplies ten different formats that can be applied to a post (not applicable to pages). The number of formats available is determined by the active theme as is the way they are implemented. A typical number is between six and eight.

For example, The Ares theme makes six available missing out Gallery, Status, Audio and Chat. Formats change the way posts look so selecting and using one or two different formats might enhance the website.

Format

- 📌 Standard
- Aside
- Image
- Video
- Audio
- Quote
- Link
- Gallery

Fig. 4.42 The various formats available in this theme.

Standard

This is the default post format and it is versatile enough to handle all types of media and images and for simplicity there is no need to use anything else.

For example, there is no need to use the Image format to include a picture in a page or post. Refer back to page 34 for a full explanation of each format type. If you are curious to see what each one might do in your chosen theme then just experiment with them.

Other Formats

To use one of the other formats you must be running an active theme that supports it.

If you really need a particular one then some help is at hand. To find a possible one go to this URL **https://en.support.wordpress.com/post-formats/** where you will find a detailed list of the formats many popular themes support.

Click on the name of the theme in the list to find if it is still actively supported. Many will be retired. Picking one from the list and just putting it into the theme search box in the Dashboard can be unsuccessful.

Using a new theme will completely change the appearance of your website but may do nothing to how each post is displayed. For a quick implementation of your website stick with the **Standard** format.

Section 9—Categories (Posts Only)

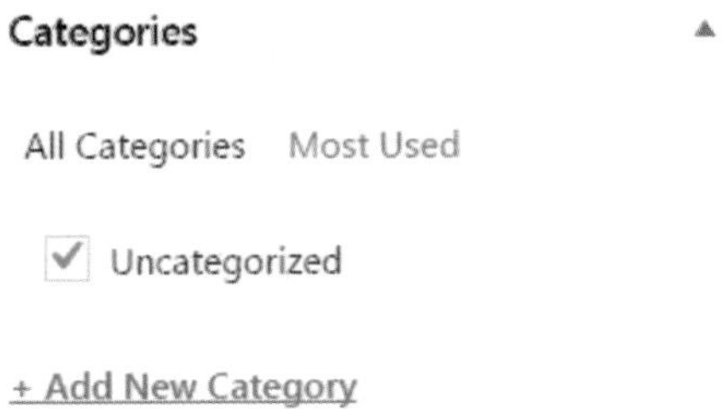

Categories   ▲

All Categories   Most Used

✔ Uncategorized

+ Add New Category

Fig. 4.43 The categories pane with the single default category.

WordPress installs itself with the single category of **Uncategorized** as shown in Figure 4.43 and every post gets this label as default. Categories help to put information into compartments so that related items can be displayed together.

It is OK to work with the default category but it could be seen as a bit 'lazy' not to have a category appropriate to the purpose of the website. Adding a new category is easy. In Figure 4.43 above is a link labelled **+Add New Category**. Just click on that to expand the section.

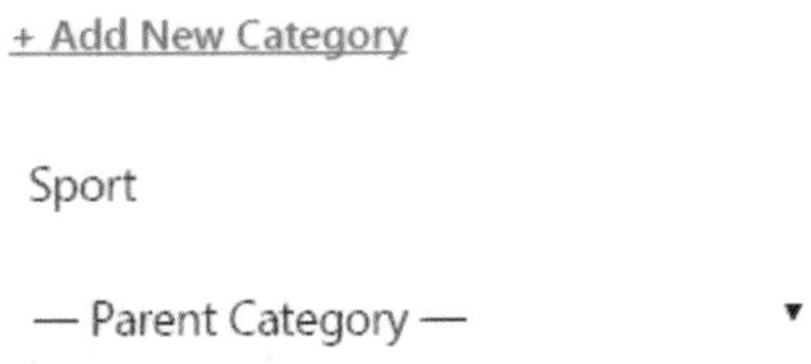

+ Add New Category

Sport

— Parent Category —   ▼

Fig. 4.44 Adding a new category of Sport to the list of categories.

Figure 4.44 illustrates the creation of a new category called Sport as a **Parent Category** or top level category. Categories can be made subordinate to other categories by selecting their parent category in that box.

Add New Category

When the new category has been named and positioned in the hierarchy click on **Add New Category** button. Next , I am going to add two subcategories of Football and Tennis as the first level down. In Figure 4.45, a nested sub-category of Football with Sport as the parent has been added and repeated for Tennis .

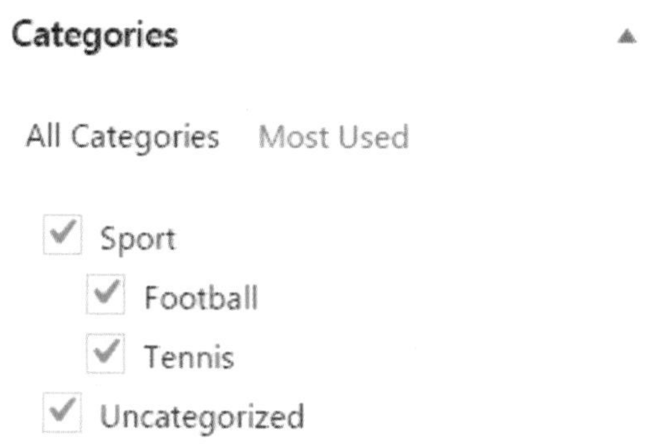

Categories   ▲

All Categories   Most Used

☑ Sport
  ☑ Football
  ☑ Tennis
☑ Uncategorized

Fig. 4.45 Here is a parent category of sport with two child categories of Football and Tennis.

There is a quirk in WordPress in that it seems to add a subordinate category to the list displayed in the box as a parent category. Exit out of the post and when it is reopened the sub-category will be in the correct place. Just like nested pages there is no absolute need to have categories or to force a structure on any categories you decide to create.

Managing Categories

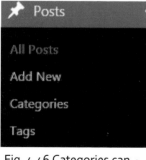

Fig. 4.46 Categories can be managed from the dashboard.

The category is the way to put some structure on a website so that users can focus on the information they are interested in. A category is essentially a filter. The categories are also available in the side menu on the dashboard under the Posts menu (Figure 4.46) and shows how many articles are in each category. It is a good way to check how many posts may have dropped into the Uncategorized category.

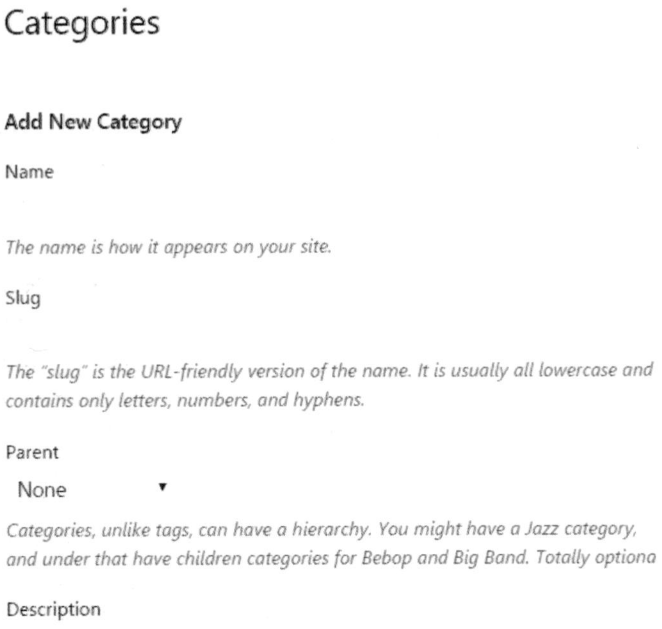

Categories

Add New Category

Name

The name is how it appears on your site.

Slug

The "slug" is the URL-friendly version of the name. It is usually all lowercase and contains only letters, numbers, and hyphens.

Parent

None   ▼

Categories, unlike tags, can have a hierarchy. You might have a Jazz category, and under that have children categories for Bebop and Big Band. Totally optiona

Description

Fig. 4.47 The Add Category screen is a bit more detailed in the dashboard menu.

Figure 4.47 shows the essential features of this area. Here it is possible to add information such as a **Slug line** that will replace the full name in the URL.

C   ⓘ wpblog.my-writing-website.co.uk/wp/category/sport/football/

Fig. 4.48 The URL with the original category.

Figure 4.48 is the original URL where the slug is football and if this is changed to footie a new URL is created as shown in Figure 4.49. This will make the original one unavailable as it has been replaced by this conversion.

C   ⓘ wpblog.my-writing-website.co.uk/wp/category/sport/footie/

Fig. 4.49 The URL has been modified by adding a slug line.

Section 10—Tags (Posts Only)

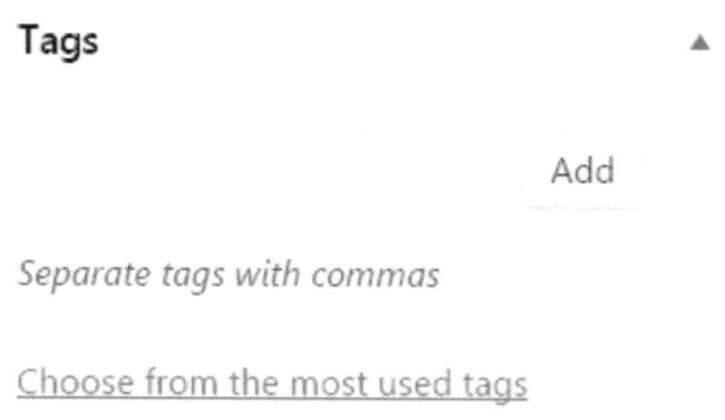

Tags   ▲

Add

Separate tags with commas

Choose from the most used tags

Fig. 4.50 WordPress starts out without any tags.

Using **Tags** is another way to add a type of filtering to a big website.

Using this feature in conjunction with categories provides lots of ways for users of the website to just view posts that interest them.

On a newly installed website there won't any tags (Figure 4.50)and clicking on the link to choose from the most used won't do anything .

Adding a New Tag

This is easy , just like adding a new category. Tags can be one word or a few words. Figure 4.51 shows two new tags added at the bottom of the post .

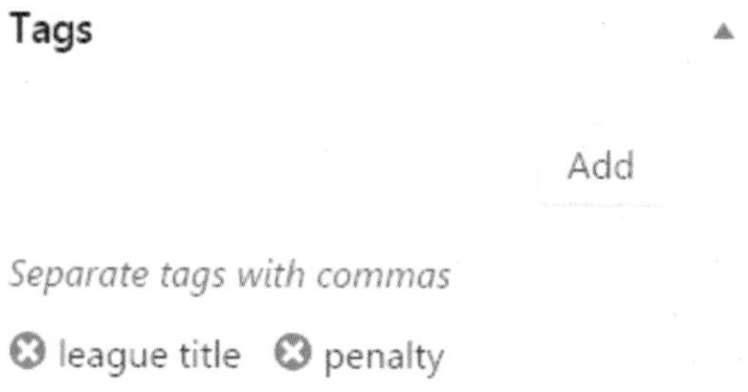

Tags   ▲

Add

Separate tags with commas

⊗ league title   ⊗ penalty

Fig. 4.51 The Tags pane with two tags added for this post.

Type the tags into the box and click **Add**. Several tags can be added at a time by separating them with commas.

Creating tags attaches them to the post being edited as well as adding them

for future use. To remove a tag from a post at any time click on

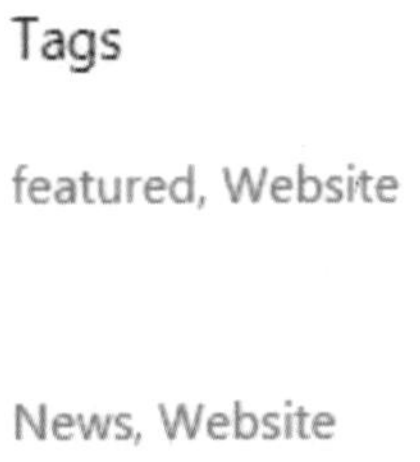

Tags

featured, Website

News, Website

Fig. 4.52 Three of the tags in use.

the x in the coloured circle and Update the post to save the changes.

If this is the only post with that tag then the tag will be removed from the database as well as the post. To find out what tags have been used open the list of **All Posts** and you will find them in the Tags column (Figure 4.52)

Here is the big difference to categories. Categories are displayed and available for every post. When adding a new post there are no tags visible and clicking on the link to **Choose from the most used tags** lists the active tags in the database.

Back on the website open a post where tags are displayed , depending on the theme, as shown in Figure 4.53. Clicking on the

kpadmin

June 19, 2017

featured, Website

Fig. 4.53Tags displayed in a Post.

Website tag brings up a list of all posts with the tag together with an extract of about 55 lines (**the excerpt**), (Figure 4.55) that will probably display many posts in their entirety.

As mentioned, the way that tags are displayed is determined by the theme. Figure 4.53 doesn't really make it clear that there are any tags. You have to rely on the curiosity of your visitors to click on the words.

Fig. 4.54 Tags as displayed in another theme.

Figure 4.54, is an image that I enhanced because the original was a very washed out grey, it is a nice display with the tags clearly highlighted.

Section 11— Excerpts (Posts Only)

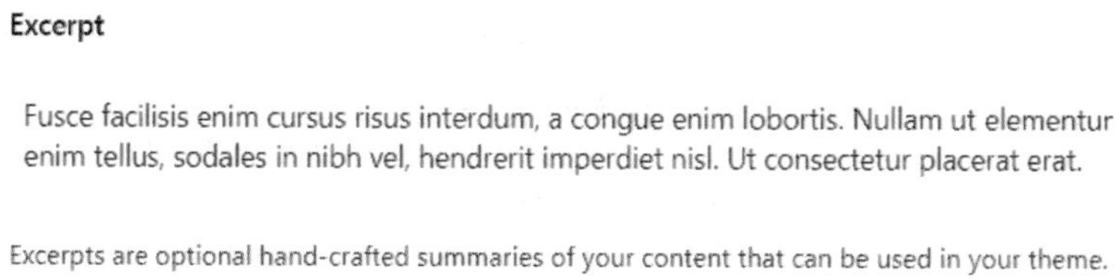

Excerpt

Fusce facilisis enim cursus risus interdum, a congue enim lobortis. Nullam ut elementur enim tellus, sodales in nibh vel, hendrerit imperdiet nisl. Ut consectetur placerat erat.

Excerpts are optional hand-crafted summaries of your content that can be used in your theme.

Fig. 4.55 The excerpt box with a summary of the post.

Sometimes **Excerpts** can save the day if the theme in use supports them but more often than not they don't. If that is the case then the only way to make the posts more compact on the home page is to use the Read More option in the editor. This means that the first few lines in the post should summarise the content with the Read More placed after that paragraph. Unfortunately there are a lot of websites that come up in a search on the topic of making the excerpt function work but most of them advocate changing the underlying code. This is both beyond the scope of this book and will probably be overwritten by every WordPress update.

A possible way forward is to use a plugin and there are a few listed. Again, your theme may inhibit its use but it is worth a try.

Easy Custom Auto Excerpt

Auto Excerpt for your post on home, search and archive. Customize Read More button and thumbnail image. Easy to configure and have a lot of options.

By tonjoo

Fig. 4.56 There are a handful of plugins but only a few are being kept up-to- date.

5

WordPress Website Appearance

The overall appearance of the website is set by the active theme. A WordPress website will always have an active theme because the software does not allow the website to operate without one.

Active: Twenty Fourteen   Customize

Fig. 5.1 The active theme is clearly indicated in WordPress.

Default Features

You are now very aware that some features on the website are set by the choice of theme. Unfortunately, you can spend many hours searching for your ideal theme. WordPress ships with a few themes as default called Twenty Fourteen, Twenty Fifteen and Twenty Sixteen. WordPress is so widely used that there are tens of thousands of themes available for you to look at.

Appearance

Themes

Customize

Widgets

Menus

Header

Background

Editor

Fig. 5.2 The Theme options are listed under the main menu item Appearance.

The vast majority of themes have a free version available for long term trials provided you acknowledge the efforts of the developer. These themes are either very simple or have a lot of functionality disabled. Download the free version and explore all the options in the trial version before paying out any money. If the developer does not offer a free or lite version then search for another one.

Getting Familiar with the Active Theme

On the administrator dashboard expand the Appearance menu entry (Figure 5.3) and click on Themes. One theme will be active with a button to Customize it.

Active: Hueman
Customize

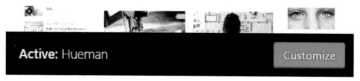

Fig. 5.3 Look for a Customize button to change the settings.

At the top of the screen note that WordPress indicates how many themes are installed, which is not that useful when there is only a small number. There may also be additional information about updates being available or that add-ons are pending (Figure 5.4).

New version available. Update now

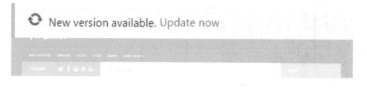

Fig. 5.4 new versions of a theme are flagged. Updates take just a few minutes to complete.

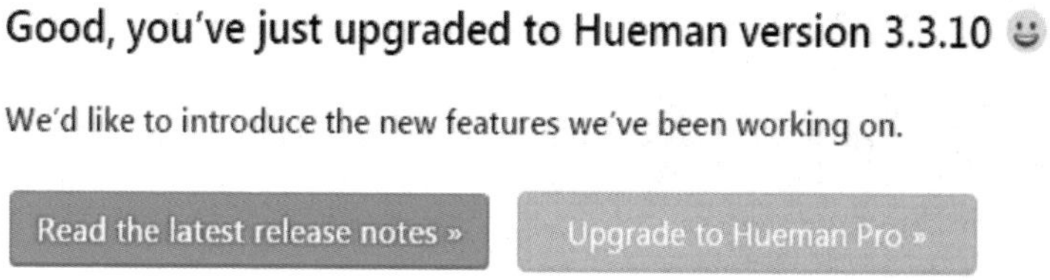

Good, you've just upgraded to Hueman version 3.3.10
We'd like to introduce the new features we've been working on.
Read the latest release notes »
Upgrade to Hueman Pro »

Fig. 5.5 The release notes contain details of what has been fixed or changed, problems being dealt with and new features.

Updating is usually OK as themes are well tested before being released and by other users. Having upgraded this particular theme provides release notes and an invitation to purchase the paid-for or Pro version (Figure 5.5).

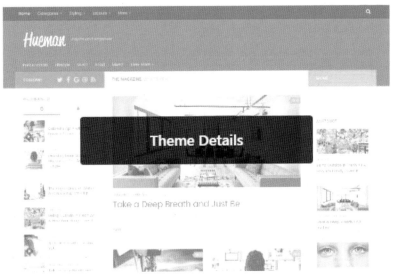

Fig. 5.6 Access the inner working of the theme to access its dashboard.

Hovering over the theme brings up a button saying Theme Details giving you a lot of information, essentially another dashboard, on the active theme. Notice that the screenshot of the theme is styled (Figure 5.7) and has content selected to make it as attractive as possible. This is the result that can be achieved but it takes work to do this and this picture is only a guide to what is possible. Creating just a few trial posts and publishing them to the website shows that the potential is clearly there. For reference this theme was developed by Hueman and found by searching the WordPress repository. The point is that this theme is very well thought out but it is not for the novice. In many ways this is a very advanced theme and one of its features is the control it offers over individual pages to make them a little different from the others. A second nice feature is that it offers views for the desktop, tablet and mobile phone.

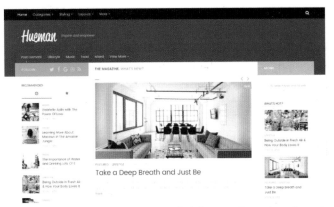

Fig. 5.7 The Hueman theme is stylish but it takes a lot of work to get it looking this good. Use it as an objective in the building of your website.

However, for the greater part of the book for discussions we will use one of the built-in WordPress themes mainly because they enable almost all the features in WordPress.

Check that the active theme is set to Twenty Sixteen (Figure 5.8) as we will mainly use this theme to demonstrate how to change and expand its various features.

Fig. 5.8 The Twenty-Sixteen theme .

Customisation

Changing the theme is called customisation and that link is in the Theme overview and on the Appearance menu.

Introduction

All themes have options for the overall web page design such as title and logo, front page content, header (the top portion of the page) and footer (the bottom portion of the page), main body (the chunk in the middle) widgets and menus.

Sometimes an item, like a banner at the top of every web page, is not in the obvious place (i.e. the header section) but could be in the main body design.

Fig. 5.9 The theme's control and status bar.

Figure 5.9 shows the top of the customizer where, from left to right, are options to go **home** (house symbol) or **exit** (large X) and usually a status icon. In this case that the theme has been saved. Changing any details will cause the icon to flip to Save and Publish and the change is previewed in the viewing pane.

There is a helpful feature indicated by a little pen to indicate where you can make quick changes and then click the button marked with the **capital X** to discard everything and not apply the changes to the website.

Fig. 5.10 The Twenty Sixteen theme with a logo, site title and tagline.

The **Twenty Sixteen** theme has editing icons dotted on the preview pane providing a shortcut to that part of the customization menu. Exiting , using the **capital X** route should return the screen to the WordPress dashboard. This brings up a slightly confusing message (Figure 5.11) about leaving this site. It doesn't mean actually exiting out of the admin pages, just away from the customization pages.

Exiting Problems

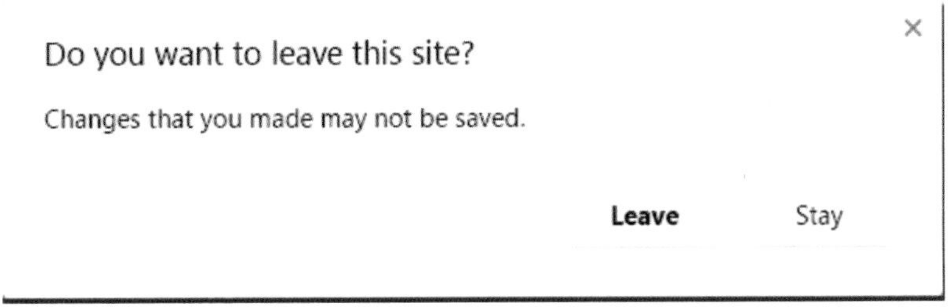

Fig. 5.11 WordPress treats the theme as a separate 'website'. This message is asking if you want to go back to the WordPress dashboard.

If clicking to **Leave** the customisation page (Figure 5.11) doesn't take you back to the WordPress dashboard it is likely that there is a problem with an installed plugin associated with the theme. The problem will probably show itself as an error message like ' **Sorry you are not allowed to access this page**' and WordPress may get itself in a loop of error messages.

Panic not, as the fix is to close the web browser or that particular tab and login again via either the primary or standby administrator account. Then go to the installed plugins and deactivate any plugins directly associated with the active theme.

Return to the customizer and try again and nine times out of ten this simple action will fix the problem. If not then it is a process of deactivating plugins one at a time until the culprit is identified. There may be an update pending for that plugin or it may be necessary to find another one to do the job.

Web Page Design

The design of the website is broken down in several areas that vary slightly between themes. There are usually two or three options listed, some of which are also found in the WordPress dashboard, to add basic branding to your website.

Site Identity

The **Twenty Sixteen** theme has three items in the section, two of which the **Site Title** and the **Tagline**, were set already in the WordPress settings. Changing the information in either place will update the other.

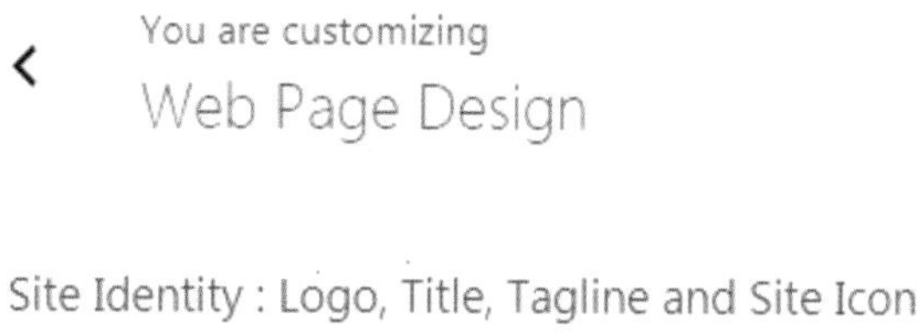

< You are customizing

Web Page Design

Site Identity : Logo, Title, Tagline and Site Icon

Fig. 5.12 The Site Identity lets the world know what your website is about.

Site Icon

Site Icon

The Site Icon is used as a browser and app icon for your site. Icons must be square, and at least **512** *pixels wide and tall.*

This is not to be confused with the Site Logo that is covered later.

The site icon is illustrated in Figure 5.13 and is a tiny image displayed in a user's browser. A nice touch but not a vital addition to a website. It is something that you can do later on.

Fig. 5.13 The Site Icon is a tiny piece of branding for your website.

Mobile Viewer

 Hide Controls

At the bottom of the customization screen are three symbols showing three sizes of viewing screen.

Fig. 5.14 Check how your website looks on mobiles.

Left to right (Figure 5.14) they are a widescreen monitor on a desktop, a 10" tablet device and a mobile phone like the iPhone. Clicking on each of these changes the preview pane to show how any change will likely be handled by one of these devices. It is not an absolute guide but will show glaring errors.

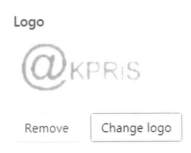

Fig. 5.15 The logo selection area.

Site Logo

The last task in this section is to upload a site logo if you want one on your website. The Twenty Sixteen theme displays this along with the site title and tagline (Figure 5.10).

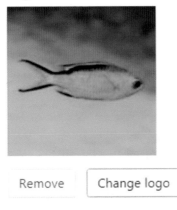

Fig. 5.16 The updated logo ready to be saved.

In Figure 5.15 I have uploaded a logo and now there are options to delete it or to change it. Click on **Change Logo** to be taken to the **Media Library.** Adding a logo for the first time will do the same thing. Choose any picture you like and click on **Select**. WordPress takes you to a Crop Image screen that has a box, of the exact dimensions, already drawn on your image. Slide the box along to the spot you want, if you need to, and then **Crop Image**. You now have a new logo ready for your website. The Preview Pane shows you what it will look like on the website. To overwrite the existing image click on **Save & Publish.**

This section is now complete for the Twenty Sixteen theme and clicking the exit arrow temporarily saves any changes and re-opens the main customization menu. As mentioned previously, if you are happy with your logo click on Save & Publish so that you don't lose the changes.

Colours or Colors

This section is to change the various colours from the default settings in the Twenty Sixteen theme. Other themes have fewer options and just let you change the Site Title colour or the background colour of the whole website. In the text I will use the UK spelling of colour even though WordPress uses the US one.

Base Colour Scheme

The Twenty Sixteen theme has five options from the Default (white) to Yellow. Try them and see what they look like.

Background Colour

Click on the Background Colour button to check the current setting or make a change. Sometimes, you can just see this as a wide edge around your web pages,

   The theme shows the colour in three ways as shown in Figure 5.17. There is the colour as displayed indicated by a white circle (you can move that around), the equivalent in a hexadecimal code, usually written as a code such as #565656 and a picker from a colour palette. The Hex colour coding system has a shortcode system for common colours and #fff is short for #ffffff that is white. On this screen the circle at the bottom left can be moved, the slider can move up and down the colour hue column or

Background Color

Fig. 5.17 The colour palette settings.

buttons select a new colour range. Select a new colour using some or all of the options. The **preview pane** reflects the changes. There is a handy **default** option to discard all your changes.

Page Background

This is the colour of the pages that sits on top of the background. In modern designs white is a good choice but feel free to change it.

Link Colour

A link is any text that takes a website visitor to another place on your website or an external website. The choice of colour is down to you and the colour picker works like all the others. Again, you have a default button to discard any changes.

Main Text Colour

Changing this setting will affect the majority of text on your website from menus to posts and pages.

 Home   Blogging Page

Fig. 5.18 All the menus are affected by the main text colour.

If you have selected a white background then black text is very effective contrast. White text on a coloured background is harder to read.

Again, trial and error is the best way to move forward.

Secondary Text Colour

Fig.5.19 The tagline is secondary text in   the Twenty Sixteen theme.

It is hard to define just what this might affect. The best thing to do is to change it to a readily identifiable colour , mauve in Figure 5.19, and scan the preview page for changes. That completes the available colour choices.

Header Image

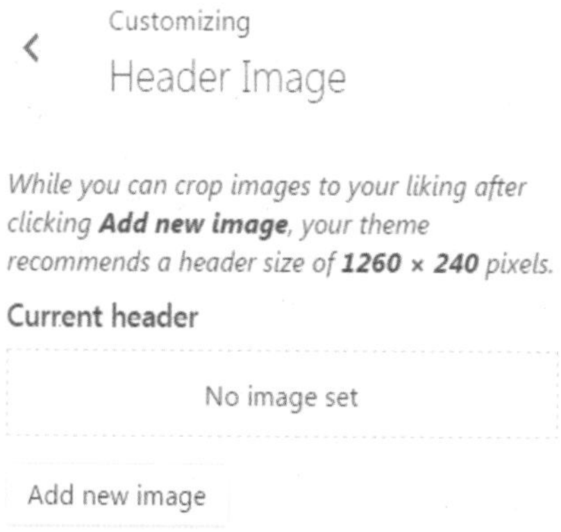

Fig. 5.20 Adding a header image is similar to adding a logo to the website.

In the Twenty Sixteen theme there is just one option and that is to add an image to the header area (Figure 5.20) of all web pages.

There is a recommended size , 1260 x 240 pixels, so ideally the header image should be a bit larger as WordPress will crop the image to the correct size.

The next step, assuming the website will have a banner in the header area is to click on the **Add new image** button.

WordPress now opens the Media Library with options to choose an image from the images already in the system or upload a new one. See Figure 5.21 and 5.22 overleaf.

WordPress carries over the suggested dimensions for a new header image. Assuming this is a new website it is likely that an image will have to be uploaded using the **Upload Files** tab.

Choose Image

Upload Files   Media Library

Fig. 5.21 Choose an image from your media Library or Upload Files from your device.

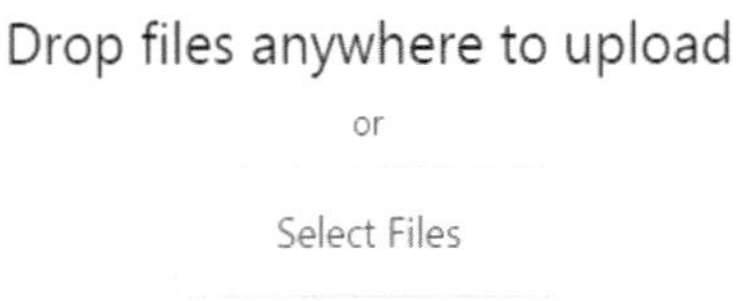

Drop files anywhere to upload

or

Select Files

Fig. 5.22 It is often easier to Select Files rather than dropping in from your device.

Using either drag and drop or clicking on Select Files to select a file on your device choose a new image. WordPress uploads the image and then provides options to edit or delete the image.

At the bottom of the screen is the quick way to just to **Select** and **Crop the Image** for use. The next screen shows the area of the uploaded image that WordPress has selected.

Part of it is in a box highlighted with squares that you drag to slide the highlighted area across the image to fine tune the crop. Once you are happy click on Crop Image and that image will become the new banner.

Current header

Hide image   Add new image

Fig. 5.23 The selected image looks good as a thumbnail but view it in the preview pane to check how it appear to the website users.

WordPress attaches other information to an image (see Figure 5.24, overleaf with some typical information added) that may not be that applicable to banner in the header .

URL	http://wpblog.my-writing-wel
Title	Banner 1
Caption	WordPress websites are easy
Alt Text	WordPress Header Image
Description	A screen grab from the writing website.

Fig. 5.24 The additional information filled out in the media library. Only the alt text is used.

If the banner has a scene or photo embedded in it then it might be worth adding a few words in the Alt Text box as most browsers display these words to a user if they cannot display the image (Figure 5.23) itself.

The description is for reference only and the caption text won't display as it is a header image.

Again, if you have any display problems they will likely be caused by the theme that may not add all the formatting to the image.

Rotating Headers

Fig. 5.25 The button shuffles your header images.

Current header

Fig. 5.26 The header image is replaced with a message.

This, toggle button selects one of the headers available when a user goes to the website . A useful feature or a novelty? Perhaps the latter in most cases.

Click the button again to stop the randomizer.

Image Editor

Permalink: http://wpblog.my-writing-website.co.uk/wp/new-header/

Fig. 5.27 The image editor with its controls.

The image editor gives you manual control over the image. This is a general image editor applicable to all images and you have probably seen it by now. The four buttons (Figure 5.27) provide rotation and mirroring of the image. Try each of them to see the effect.

Scale Image

Original dimensions 1754 × 144

New dimensions:

1754 × 144   Scale

Fig. 5.28 Scale the image but do note that the aspect ratio is not locked.

good help that is accessed by clicking on the Question Mark.

The best way to get familiar with this tool is to play with it . A pixel is a small dot, in fact the smallest element that makes up an image. The aspect ratio is the ratio of the width to the height of an image.

There is also a column with option to Scale the image using pixels (px) that can be more useful that cropping it.

Also available is an Image Crop function. Both options have

Image Crop

Aspect ratio:

:

Selection:

×

Fig. 5.29 The crop tool. Do read the help file.

Background Image

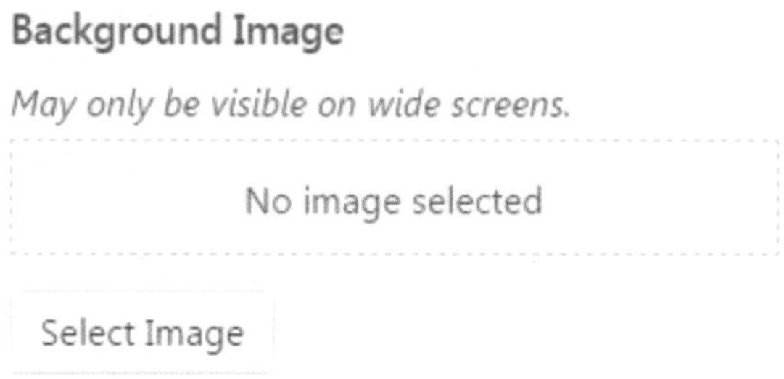

Background Image

May only be visible on wide screens.

No image selected

Select Image

Fig. 5.30 Start by selecting an image from the Media Library.

A similar screen to the one in the previous section. The problem here is that the image may not show except in the right sidebar of widescreen devices.

If you changed the background colour and couldn't detect any change then it is likely that the background is off the edge of the screen. The Twenty Sixteen theme is set to a fixed width of 1260px. Even if you choose to discard the image later select one so that the image controls section makes sense to you.

Image Controls

Preset

Default

Image Position

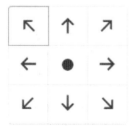

There are additional controls here to control the position of the image (Figure 5.31)and how it fits on the screen. The first is **Preset** where the options are **Default** (let WordPress do the work), **Fill Screen** (stretch the image), **Fit to Screen** (scale the image down), **Repeat** (tile the screen) and **Custom** (settings you choose).

The Default option is set so the rest of the options adopt their default positions. The image is smaller than the screen so WordPress is going to Repeat the Background image (box ticked) starting in the top right hand corner indicated by the arrow.

Fig. 5.31 The soft joystick.

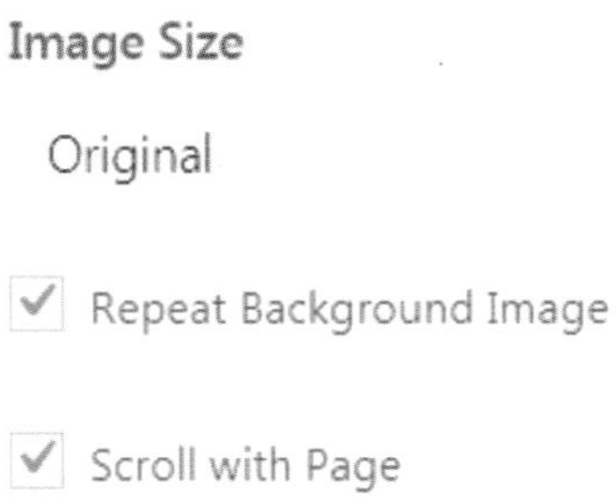

Image Size

Original

✓ Repeat Background Image

✓ Scroll with Page

Fig. 5.32 The rest of the controls on the default setting.

To see the effect click Save & Publish and if your screen is wide enough there will be an area tiled with the image (Figure 5.32). Experiment with the other settings to learn their effects as other Presets remove some of the options shown in Figure 5.32.

These settings have very limited value in some themes like the Twenty Fourteen one, but the image is just detectable in the Twenty Sixteen theme around the edge of the screen. You can use it to produce a nice effect.

Menus

A menu is a route to your content and expanding the item lists the menu locations available in the theme and under that are the menus that you have created.

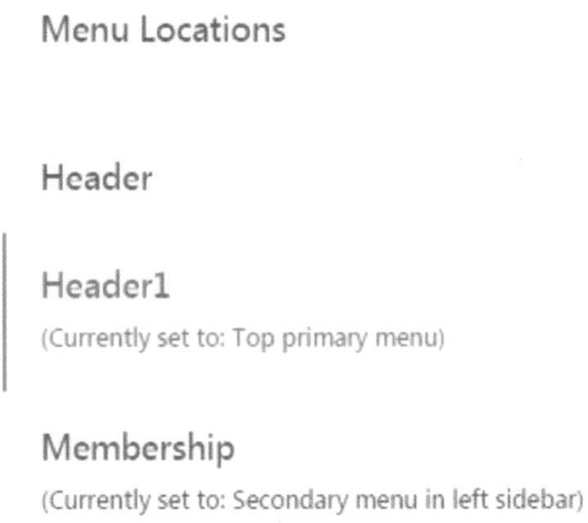

Menu Locations

Header

Header1
(Currently set to: Top primary menu)

Membership
(Currently set to: Secondary menu in left sidebar)

Fig. 5.33 The menu selection screen with some menus already set up.

On a new site WordPress will have a default menu. There will be details on how many menus the theme supports (Twenty Sixteen has just two), where they are located and which menu occupies the location. The Twenty Sixteen theme, like many others, won't stack menus on top of each other and if you try to do that it will swap the two menus. A **widget**, more on these later, can be used to add another menu to the web pages. Menu management is available in depth using the Menu item in the dashboard sidebar. Expanding a menu by clicking on it reveals the items or page/post links in that menu (Figure 5.34). Clicking on the down arrow to the right of the word Page or Post expands that single item (Figure 5.35) to show the navigation label, that you can edit by overtyping the word in the box plus an option to remove the entry in the menu.

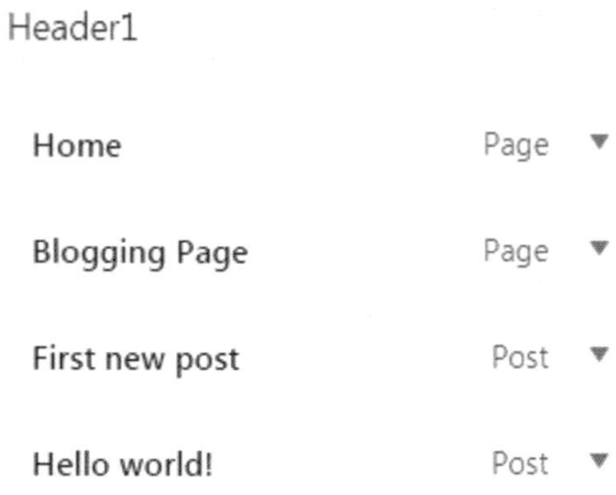

Header1

Home   Page   ▼

Blogging Page   Page   ▼

First new post   Post   ▼

Hello world!   Post   ▼

Fig. 5.34 The expanded menu with details of posts and pages.

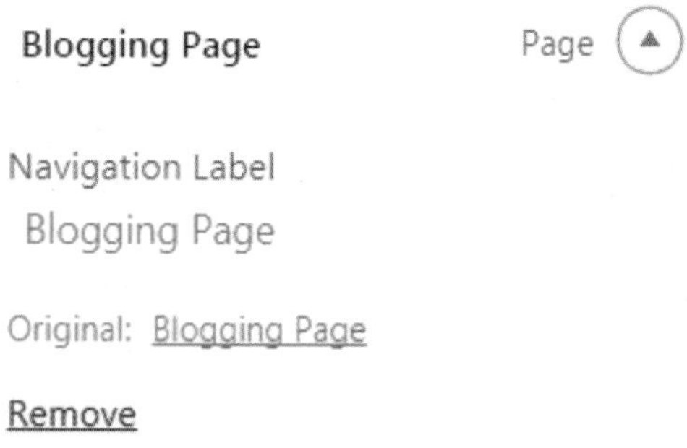

Blogging Page   Page   ⏶

Navigation Label
Blogging Page

Original: Blogging Page

Remove

Fig. 5.35 The expanded menu item.

Reorder   ➕ Add Items

Fig. 5.36 Down at the bottom of the menu listing are options to re-order, add items and delete the whole menu.

Figure 5.36 shows the rest of the controls. The first is to **reorder** the menu items, perhaps in order of their importance. Next is a button to add fresh items to the menu and not shown is an option to delete the menu completely. Back a page, on Figure 5.33, there is an option to **Add a Menu** that I have not shown because I wanted to take you through the menus in a logical way.

Even though there is a separate dashboard item it is possible to do all the basic menu tasks in the theme.

Widgets

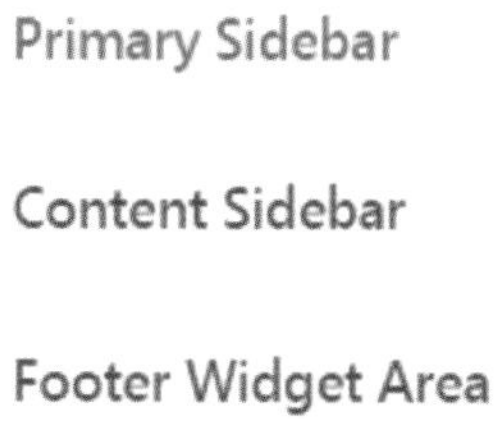

Primary Sidebar

Content Sidebar

Footer Widget Area

Fig. 5.37 Some of the widget positions.

Widgets are mini plugins that add functionality to the website. There is a Widget menu on the dashboard and the one in the theme shows you where they are located.

Expanding any of three areas lists the active widgets and allows deletion and re-ordering.

Static Front Page

This section is the same as the one in the General Settings in the dashboard and changes in one are mirrored in the other.

Additional CSS

CSS, or Cascading Style Sheets, complements HTML and other programming languages. CSS lets a programmer create central style sheets that every web page can use. Before CSS any change in style, like using a larger font in the menu, had to be re-coded on every web page. With CSS the code refers to a style sheet and once that is changed every web page is updated automatically.

For the beginner adding CSS, even snippets from the internet, is fraught with danger and best avoided.

Featured Content

Some themes have an option for posts to be given a prominent position on your website. The posts can be laid out in grid or in slider but they have to be given a tag called Featured and you should change this if it clashes with a tag you set up.

This option can be another distraction in WordPress where you spend a lot of time for little gain so park it for a rainy day.

The Themes in Summary

I selected Twenty Sixteen to explain a theme's features and functions but one of the others might suit your needs.

Twenty Fourteen

This is a very basic theme and it does have limitations. The header image is large, background colours and images are either invisible or off to the right-hand side and there are only two menus available. Use Twenty Fourteen to teach yourself how basic customisation works and what is possible, but use it with caution.

Twenty Fifteen and Twenty Sixteen

Twenty Fifteen still has issues especially with where the header and background images are located. Twenty Sixteen is better once you accept that the top menu is above the header image. Depending on your design objectives this can look a bit funny. The content is centrally placed rather than aligned to the left.

Twenty Seventeen

Twenty Seventeen launched in 2017 and is a more modern style but has a very large picture on the home page. You can download it from the WordPress repository.

Notes on your Site Logos

These themes bring in a new concepts such as a site logo, as they move forward with time. When you add the logo WordPress will open the media library and you will have to upload it if it is not already on the website. Usefully WordPress next moves on to the option is to crop the image if that helps. One of the problems that I have found with some themes is that it is assumed that the logo contains the same information as the Site Title and the logo overwrites the text with the image. If you really like a theme and want a logo as well as the site title then the only option may be to add a banner or header image containing the logo.

General Design Options

Some commercial themes have more customisation options and I will try to cover as many as possible in broad terms. The theme will list the areas covered by this section but usually it is fonts and colours. If you are not sure what to do then stick with the defaults but the theme will let you experiment without affecting the live website and you can always quickly undo your changes.

Fonts

The font is the typeface used for the characters on the website. A lot has been written about safe fonts to use on the internet. Safe means those fonts that will display clearly on a wide variety of equipment.

Fonts are classified into four broad families of serif, sans-serif, cursive (like handwriting) and monospace. A serif is an embellishment added to a letter.

The letter g from the Calibri font in Word has a short horizontal line on the top of the letter that may be blurred in a small size font on a poor quality screen. This type of font is fine for documents meant to be downloaded and printed but for a website choose a font without this feature. These fonts are called sans-serif. A very safe font to use is Arial sans-serif but also widely used are Helvetica, Times New Roman sans-serif, Microsoft Sans Serif, Courier New and Tahoma.

See how each font looks before setting it as the default one for your website. The monospace and cursive fonts are used to achieve visual effects on websites. Monospace are like the typewriters of old that allocate the same space or width to each letter. Cursive fonts might be useful for things like menus or invitations.

Default Font Size

If there is an option to change the default font size it might be worth considering. The default font size will be determined by factors such as the target audience or an effect to add to the visual appeal of the web pages. As a guide the minimum font size should be 14pt. This is the default character size if no other styling is applied.

Max Width of the Website

The theme may offer this as a setting and usually will give you guidance on what to choose. This will be linked to the number of sidebars you are setting up. A sidebar is a column either to the left or the right of the main body.

Some themes offer four columns but most often it is three. Your website doesn't need to have any sidebars and you can work out the best setting by trial and error.

The widgets on the website may influence your choice but if you are only using a few, like a calendar, then they might fit comfortably in the footer area.

Colours

As always, these options are theme dependent. If in doubt then stay with the default settings. If colour is important then the web is a great source of how to combine colours to achieve a particular effect. For a natural look then ochres , greens and blues may be the combination to work with. A sports club might want to use the team's colours.

Background Image

This topic has been covered with the Twenty Fourteen through Twenty Seventeen themes but here are some ideas to consider. A background image might enhance your web pages provided it doesn't overwhelm your content and make it difficult to read.

The image can be big enough to fill the whole background of the web page or, if much smaller, can be set to tile the background both horizontally and vertically.

If you are building a website for the first time then I recommend that you ignore this feature. Many websites have a clean look with a white or off-white background.

Header Design

Here you will discover other options, some of which may turn out to be the same as those in previous sections, to change the content of the header area. For example, I have found that a number of themes just go back to the Site Identity section where we encountered the problem with the logo. The header area is likely to be split into three areas, some of which may not be visible at this stage because you haven't added menus or other pieces of information. There may also be an option to set a different colour for the mobile menu, even though it is hard to see why you might want to do this.

Header Menus

A very important section that will make your website come alive. You may have to go back to a previous header section to adjust your colour scheme.

Topbar Menu

If there is an option to create a default menu then apply it for the moment as this will let you view the position, colour and fonts. The menu can be changed and adjusted later as content is added to the website.

Menu Settings

Usually menus are always visible at the top of the page and the content scrolls underneath it but sometimes a nice effect can be achieved by hiding the menu while scrolling down and then revealing it when the user starts to scroll back up.

Select each setting in turn to see what actually happens as some settings may do the same thing while others may not match your understanding of the words.

Mobile Content

Because so many users have mobile devices and this is really anything portable such as tablets of various sizes and mobile telephones, mobile now has a high important in the online world especially with the search engines.

It may be worth considering if there should be a separate menu for mobile users that looks better on smaller screens.

Main Body Content

This will usually include the content area and the sidebars. If not there should be a separate section for the sidebars. The content will typically be defined as three columns comprising the sidebars and the wider middle column for text and images.

Sometimes the theme lets you shuffle the columns to move the content to the left or right. Not all designs look good but you can try them all out at your leisure .

Problems might arise with plugins that don't adapt with fluid layouts. It may also be possible to adjust the layout for a small selection of different pages.

A word of advice. Don't change several settings at once or you are likely to get lost and spend hours trying to get the web pages back to the default. Just change one at a time and do make notes that you can refer back to with the date added.

Single Post Settings

This section tailors how single posts look when opened from a list. There should be options to use the default format for the mainbody content or change it to one of the available formats. For example, if the post is packed with information then removing the sidebars will allow more reading space on the screen.

Navigation

Moving between previous and next posts is usually via Previous and Next buttons. A small number of themes give control of how this works and how the buttons or characters look.

Footer Region

This area of the website can often be overlooked but it can be used for a lot of important information especially if you need to display terms and conditions or other commercial or legal information.

WordPress assumes that this region will comprise almost entirely of widgets. We will cover widgets in more detail shortly but they are small code blocks that perform a particular function.

Depending on the theme you may be able to split the footer area into as many as four columns, add another menu to that region, change the colour and possibly add your logo which can be difficult to do in the header area.

If no widgets are enabled then the footer region will not change.

Notes on Menus

As mentioned, menus are probably the most important navigation aid on your website. When you start to customize your theme you ,most likely, will not see any menus on your website. The theme may allow you to enable default menus that will help you with your design. The most common menu names are listed but you will encounter others. Enable them with a menu item and see where they show up. An empty menu will not be displayed.

Topbar Menu—As the name indicates, this menu is located at the very top of each web page.

Header Menu — Located in the header region and the exact location varies with the theme.

Footer Menu — In the lower part of the screen area usually above any widgets.

Adding a new Menu

We now move on in our general discussion of themes to create a new menu of our own. In the customisation section of the theme (**Appearance** menu on the dashboard) open the **Customize** option and then the **Menu** option. Later, we will use the Menu option itself to manage our menus. After clicking on the **Add a Menu** button we need to come up with a name for it and it seems sensible to label it with *Header* or *Header1* if it is a new menu for that region.

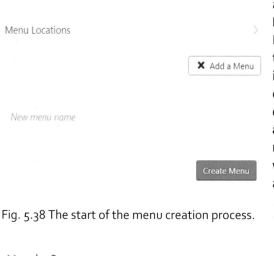

Menu Locations

✕ Add a Menu

New menu name

Create Menu

Fig. 5.38 The start of the menu creation process.

Header2

➕ Add Items

Fig. 5.39 Stage two is to Add Items to the menu.

After clicking or tapping on **Create Menu,** see Figure 5.38, the next step is to add some items to our menu, as shown in Figure 5.39. Remember that you may only have a few pages on your website and you might have to quickly exit the theme to create one or two more.

Deleting a Menu

Menus can be deleted if they get in a mess or if you are just practicing how to do it. Open the Menus section and click on the name of the menu that you want to delete. This expands into a summary of the menu including links and location. There will be options to **Delete Menu** and to **Reorder** the items it contains. Click on the delete option and it will be deleted without any prompt to check if you are sure you want to do this.

Don't forget that if you have made a mistake just exit out of the customisation without saving the changes to keep the old settings.

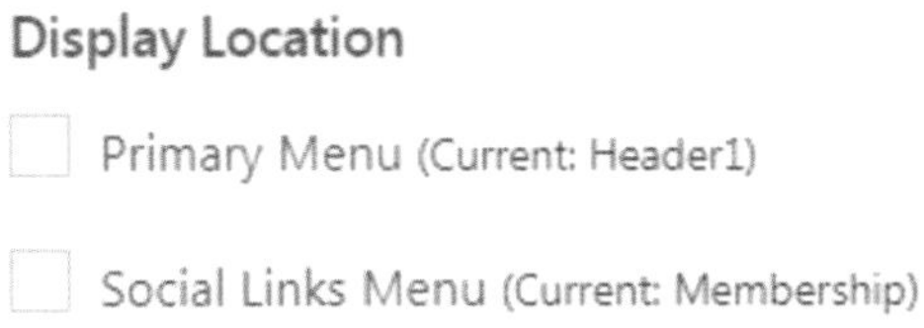

Display Location

Primary Menu (Current: Header1)

Social Links Menu (Current: Membership)

Fig. 5.40 The Twenty Sixteen menu only has two menu locations.

On the same pane will be a list of the available locations for your new menu. Remember that if you select a location that already has a menu your original menu will be displaced.

Social Media Menu

Fig. 5.41 A social media menu.

Some themes claim to support two menus and one of them might be a social links menu. The customisation section indicates that you can put any menu in this region. However, all you can do is add custom links to social media sites and nothing else will work. Figure 5.41 is the social media menu in the Twenty Sixteen theme with two links.

The Facebook one picks up the correct icon but the second internet link to the BBC is only given a default icon. Links to internal items such as pages and posts are not displayed on the live website even though they will be shown in the live preview pane in the Customisation menu.

Adding Menu Items

We are still working with the Twenty Sixteen theme and now know that the only menu locations available to you in the Primary Menu. Now click on the **Add Items** as shown in Figure 5.39. With this particular theme a submenu opens in an accordion like

Pages

Posts

Lightbox Gallery

Custom Links

Categories

Fig. 5.42 You can add items (links) in your menu to almost everything on your website.

fashion to let you select almost everything on your website and custom links to other websites. See Figure 5.42.

Experiment with Menus

The only way to understand menus is to create them, add some links to see where they appear, delete and reorder them. Use all the item types listed to see how they are added to a menu and how screens change with each type. Figure 5.43 is an example of adding a post to your menu. To get that input box click on Posts as shown in Figure 5.42. Put some text in the box that will appear on your menu , click on the post it will open (the + will change to a ✓) and last of all click on the **+ Add** button. You have just added a new item to your menu. Continue in the same way to add links to pages, categories, etc. When you are done remember to **Save & Publish** it to your website.

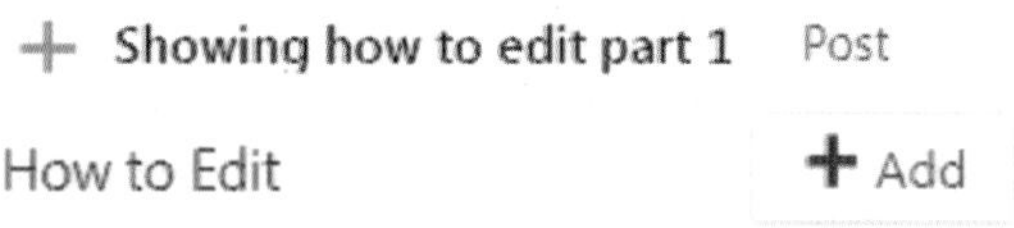

╈ Showing how to edit part 1   Post

How to Edit   **+** Add

Fig. 5.43 Adding a post to a menu.

Another thing to do is to create menus in one theme and then to switch to another theme to see what happens.

With the WordPress supplied themes you may not see any difference. Try swapping to a commercial theme such as *Hueman* or *Ares* with several menu locations to see what difference they make.

If you are sticking with a simple theme for the moment then you can also place menus in **widget areas** with the "Custom Menu" widget. Widgets are covered in Chapter 6.

6

WordPress Widgets

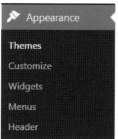

All themes implement the widgets provided by the WordPress software. The theme will enable some widgets as a matter of course but these can be removed or repositioned to suit your needs. Widgets are part of the Appearance menu as shown in Figure 6.1.

Fig. 6.1 The Widgets menu.

Widget Positions

This varies a little bit with each theme but widgets have a number of pre-defined areas such as the footer and the sidebars (Figure 6.2). There will be primary and secondary positions located in the left and right sidebars respectively.

Get to the widgets directly via the dashboard menu item or via the theme customisation section to access any additional features.

You are customizing

Widgets

Sidebar

Content Bottom 1

Content Bottom 2

Fig. 6.2 Some widget positions.

Hueman Theme

The Hueman theme enables six widgets in the left sidebar that can appear on right hand side of your page if you change the main body content layout.

Ares Theme

This theme is very different with just a few places to add widgets. They are the header area, the mainbody and the footer. All these areas are full width.

Twenty Sixteen Theme

This theme has three places to add widgets, one in the sidebar and two at the bottom which is the footer area. Going up or down in the number of widget areas available will alter your website and probably mess it up. Start with a few widgets until you have settled on a theme and you will save yourself a lot of work.

Changing the Widgets

There are two ways to get to the website's widgets. They are available on the dashboard under Appearance that provides a complete overview of what is used. They will also appear in the theme's customization section and will probably give you a slightly different picture of how many have been implemented in the theme. As we found out before with the post types the theme may suppress some of the features in WordPress.

The theme may also remove widget positions if the mainbody content layout has been reduced from the expected three column layout.

The Hueman theme, for example, hides the secondary widget position if the right sidebar has not been used. Figure 6.3 lists just the primary and four footer locations when the mainbody content is set to two column with the content on the left. The secondary widget position is available when the three-column layout is selected. The theme has an option to **Create and Manage widget zones** where you can create a second layer of widget zones below the original four as shown in Figure 6.4 where Footer 5 sits below Footer 4.

Primary

Footer 1

Footer 2

Footer 3

Footer 4

Create and manage widget zones

Fig. 6.3 A theme will reduce the number of widget positions if you change the layout too much.

Fig. 6.4 Clever themes let you stack the widgets.

This lets you become really creative with your website design.

Make Notes

Do make copious and detailed notes on what you learn and the changes you make as it is difficult to remember it all later.

The Widgets in Detail.

The next few pages are a guide to the widgets in WordPress. You will understand this section better if you open the **Widgets** menu that is under **Appearance**. On one side of the screen are a list of widgets and on the other the a list of locations.

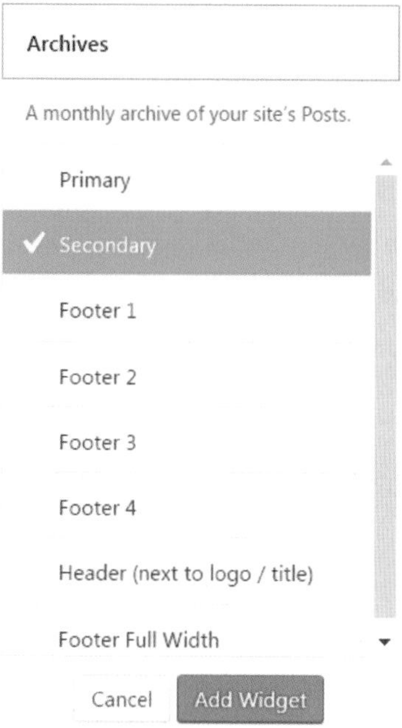

Widgets are enabled or disabled by dragging or dropping them to and from the parking area to the widget positions. They can also be deactivated by opening them and clicking the delete option. The widgets can also be given new titles. If drag and drop doesn't work for you then click on the widget in the list of widgets to open up a list of available positions. Select the position you want and then start to configure any options.

Fig. 6.5 Adding the Archives widget to the Secondary widget position.

Archives

Archives (Figure 6.5) provides a list of old posts on the website. As with all widgets it can have a new

Archives

Title:

☐ Display as dropdown
☑ Show post counts

Fig. 6.6 Give the widget a title and choose how to display the posts.

ARCHIVES

- July 2017
- June 2017
- May 2017
- March 2017
- December 2016

Fig. 6.7 Month by month archives.

title. The widget has two options that are well described.

The widget has one drawback. As it is implemented it will keep adding months to the list and extending the space used on the web page. This is not too bad if the widget is in the footer area as it will just distort the symmetry of the website.

If placed in one of the sidebars the widget will push the other items down the list. The only other option available is to select to display the list as a dropdown menu (Figure 6.6).

Figure 6.7 shows the archives in the footer area listied month by month. Figure 6.8 is the widget with a new title and the dropdown menu to select a month. Note that using the dropdown menu option duplicates the title of the widget.

It is possible to limit the number of months shown but that involves editing the programme used to drive the widget and this is beyond the scope of this book. The exact implementation is governed by the space available in the overall website design.

OLDER ENTRIES

Select Month   ▼

Fig. 6.8 A more compact style to select a month.

Calendar

This widget creates a calendar to show every day on which an article was added to the website. The calendar uses a familiar layout with each day a post was added highlighted in a different colour and inactive months are skipped in the previous/next month slider at the bottom.

June 2017

M	T	W	T	F	S	S
			1	2	3	4
5	6	7	8	9	10	11
12	13	14	15	16	17	18
19	20	21	22	23	24	25
26	27	28	29	30		

« May   Jul »

Fig. 6.9 The calendar picks up its style from the theme.

Apart from changing the title to possibly avoid confusion with future events there are no other options for this widget.

The widget picks up the styling from the theme as shown in Figure 6.9

Categories

This widget simply lists all the categories on the website including the default one of **Uncategorised**. If there is a hierarchy to the categories then it can be displayed. Figure 6.10 shows the widget on the website page and Figure 6.11 is the widget configuration where the title is editable and the space occupied by the widget can be decreased by using a dropdown menu. You can also show the number of posts in each category as well as a hierarchy.

OUR CATEGORIES

• Uncategorized

Fig. 6.10 As displayed.

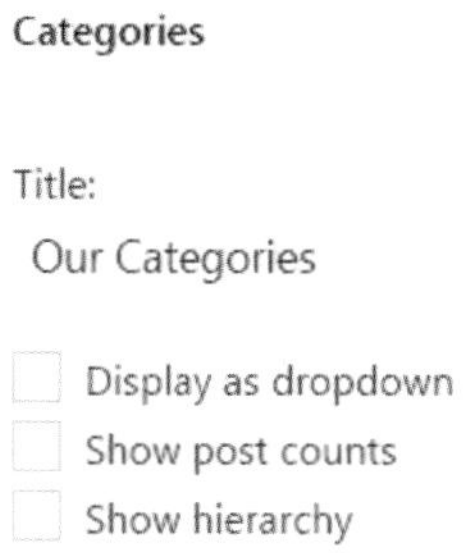

Categories

Title:

Our Categories

☐ Display as dropdown
☐ Show post counts
☐ Show hierarchy

Fig. 6.11 The options for the widget.

Be careful with this as there is a fixed width available in the widget column and the results may not be as expected.

Custom Menu

This is a very useful widget as it gives you a way to add another menu to the website to overcome the problem with the number of items on the header menu due to the lack of locations to place it on the web page. Useful as this widget is, it is very difficult to add a second widget-based custom menu but later in the book you will find out how to create nested menus. The option screen is shown in Figure 6.12.

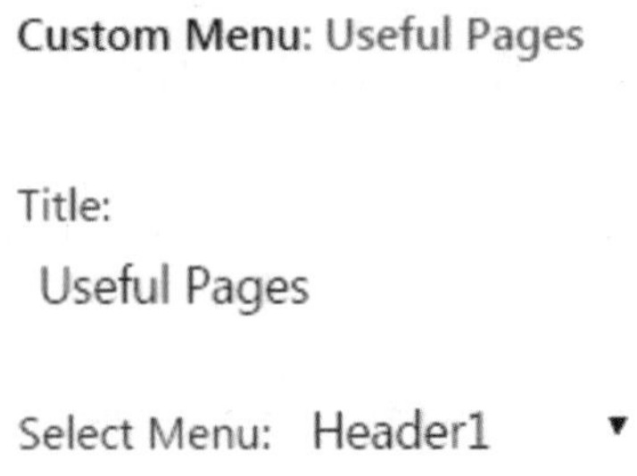

Custom Menu: Useful Pages

Title:

Useful Pages

Select Menu: Header1   ▼

Fig. 6.12 The custom menu needs a title and a menu name to work.

Meta

This is the default widget used by WordPress if there are no other menus or widgets enabled. Only two of the five entries are really useful, **register** and **login,** but they and others can only be removed by editing the underlying code. The other ways are to install a plugin or add those useful links in a menu.

Pages

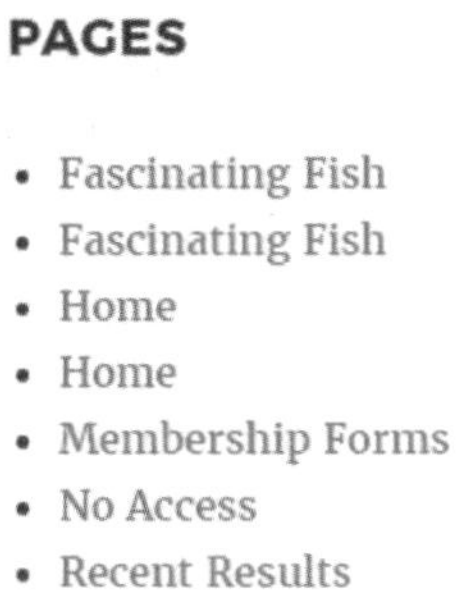

PAGES

- Fascinating Fish
- Fascinating Fish
- Home
- Home
- Membership Forms
- No Access
- Recent Results

Fig. 6.13 The pages listed by Page Title.

The pages widget is great for adding a selection of pages to your website. The widget will look at all your pages and you can sort them by **Page Title**, **Page Order** or **Page ID**. Picking the widget's default settings, and with just a few pages so far on the website the output 'menu' looks like Figure 6.13 where **all** the pages in WordPress are listed in alphabetical order.

The widget doesn't offer any way to limit the list to a specific number of pages in the system. Using the next sort option, **Page Order** as shown in Figure 6.14, will probably make no difference to the list unless each page is edited to give it an **order number**.

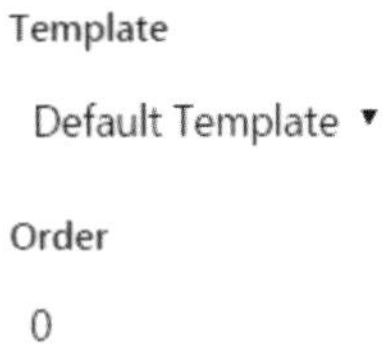

Template

Default Template ▼

Order

0

Fig. 6.14 Page editor with the Order field.

To use this feature you need to set the page order manually in the Page Attributes of each page on your website using the page editor.

Here you get more control over the order your pages appear in. The default value for every page is zero so WordPress then uses a default sort option of the title in descending alphabetical order.

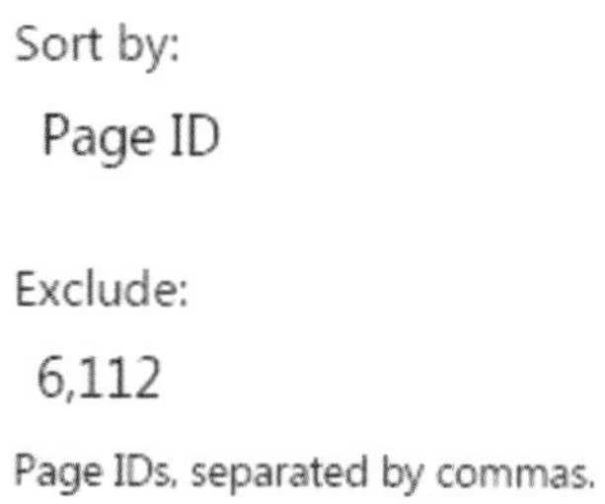

Sort by:

Page ID

Exclude:

6,112

Page IDs, separated by commas.

Fig. 6.15 Sorting by Page ID is more complicated to do.

The final option is to sort by **Page ID.** Each piece of information in WordPress has an ID and to be search engine friendly WordPress has made every effort to hide it without updating their widgets.

In Figure 6.15 there are two page IDs in the exclude list, 6 and 112, and saving those settings will eliminate two pages from the widget. So how do you find the page ID?

In the dashboard click on Pages to bring up the list of pages on the website. Click on the title of any of the pages as if you were going to edit it and in the URL address bar you will see a complicated URL like this.

ⓘ wpblog.my-writing-website.co.uk/wp/wp-admin/post.php?post=6&action=edit

Look along this string of data and you will see '?post=6'. This particular page has an internal ID of 6.

To understand this a bit better pick the next page in your list of pages and do the same thing. Chances are that this will have a page ID that is not even close to the last one. You cannot rely on using a 'one-up' method to figure out the ID of pages.

The Pages widget can be used in another menu to make a small number of pages available to your web users. Just change the title of the widget to a meaningful name.

Recent Comments

RECENT COMMENTS

- kpadmin on Second Post – no comments
- kpadmin on Fascinating Fish
- kpadmin on Second Post – no comments
- kpadmin on First new post
- kpadmin on First new post

Fig. 6.16 The list of the five most recent comments.

As the name suggests this adds a list of recent comments posted on your website as shown in Figure 6.16. Unlike other lists that just grow with the size of the website the widget has an option to limit the number of comments with the default set at 5.

The number can be altered to whatever limit you want. See Figure 6.17 for the options for this widget. I don't believe that there is an upper limit.

Recent Comments

Title:

Number of comments to show: 5

Fig. 6.17 The number of comments set to 5.

Recent Posts

The settings for this widget are familiar as they are almost the same as those for Recent Comments.

RECENT POSTS

- How to Edit
  July 12, 2017
- June Updates
  June 19, 2017
- Website Updates
  June 13, 2017

Fig. 6.18 Recent posts and dates.

Accepting the widget defaults and leaving the title unchanged, only the last three posts will be listed and each one will also have the date it was posted. Note that the widget has picked up the secondary text colour from the theme's setting.

RSS

RSS stands for Really Simple Syndication and is a link to a page on a website that provides a feed of stories for use by other sites.

RSS was very popular but is now declining as people use Facebook and Twitter feeds. RSS might add a nice feature such as local weather if you run a sports club or news items from a similar organisation. The best way is to find RSS feeds is via an internet

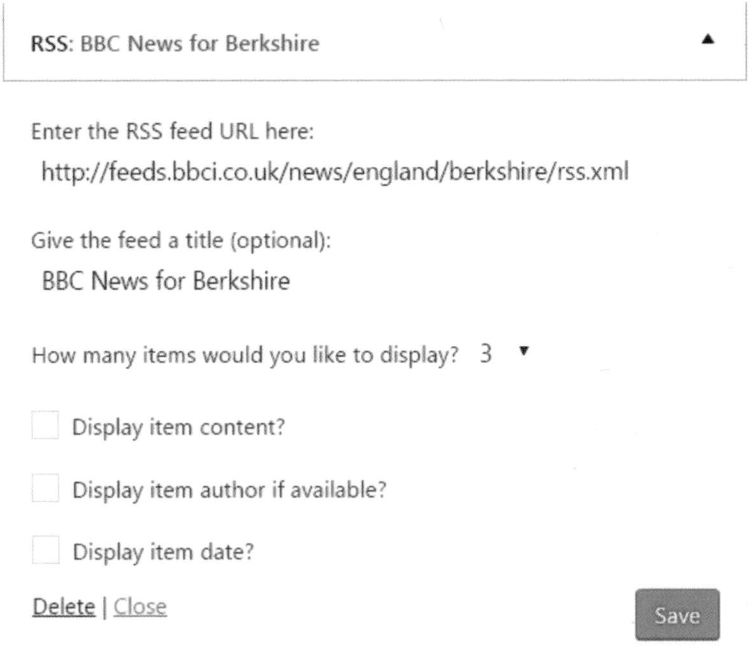

RSS: BBC News for Berkshire   ▲

Enter the RSS feed URL here:

http://feeds.bbci.co.uk/news/england/berkshire/rss.xml

Give the feed a title (optional):

BBC News for Berkshire

How many items would you like to display?   3   ▼

☐ Display item content?

☐ Display item author if available?

☐ Display item date?

Delete | Close   Save

Fig. 6.19 The RSS widget is one with the most options.

search. The feed page will usually provide the URL to copy and paste into the boxes as shown in Figure 6.19. The URL should be like the one shown in Figure 6.19 ending in rss.xml otherwise it will not work.

This is a sample entry from BBC local sports news.

BBC NEWS FOR BERKSHIRE

Jake Hyde: Maidenhead United sign Stevenage striker from 1 July

Search

 There is probably a search symbol, it looks like a magnifying glass, in the header area or on the top menu. It can vary from just an icon to a search box depending on the theme.

Fig. 6.20 A typical search box. Others have different words.

The search widget lets you add another one in a sidebar or footer. The only setup option is to add a custom title over the search box.

Tag Cloud

A tag cloud is a type of graphic based on the tags you have set in the system, that shows how often they have been used by the size of the letters. The theme determines how the cloud is displayed as shown in Figure 6.21.

Fig. 6.21 Types of tag clouds.

The sizing is a relative measure but the names of the tag won't keep growing indefinitely. The entries in the tag cloud are links to those tags or categories and clicking on them open up a list of articles.

The widget has three options in the menu under **taxonomy**. **Tags** and **Categories** are familiar and you can see how they work by swopping them over and Saving the widget. **Link categories** need a little more explanation by going back to the WordPress dashboard. Clicking on the **Links** menu expands it and also lists any links set up in the database. At this stage it is likely that the list will be empty.

Fig. 6.22 Link categories are in the Links menus.

To demonstrate how the links work I have created two links associated with football, the Football Association shortened to FA and the Premier League.

If you want to add some links of your own then carefully follow the instructions and tick the link categories that apply to each one.

There are a couple of new concepts here. The first one is the **Target**, which means the target of the link, and then to control how it opens. The end result depends a little on how your visitor's browser is configured. The choice is between opening the link either as a new website (**_blank**) taking your visitor away from your website or as another instance of the browser or an additional tab in the open browser (**_none**).

Target

> _blank — new window or tab.
>
> _top — current window or tab, with no frames.
>
> _none — same window or tab.

Choose the target frame for your link.

Fig. 6.23 A target determines how the link will be displayed in the user's browser.

With the latter your website is still open on the PC or tablet and is usually the best option to keep your website in front of the web user. Shy away from using the **_top** option as it can be a little unpredictable.

Then there are two other areas that you can safely ignore. **Link relationships (XFN)** where any '**none**' options should be ticked and **Advanced** that can be left blank.

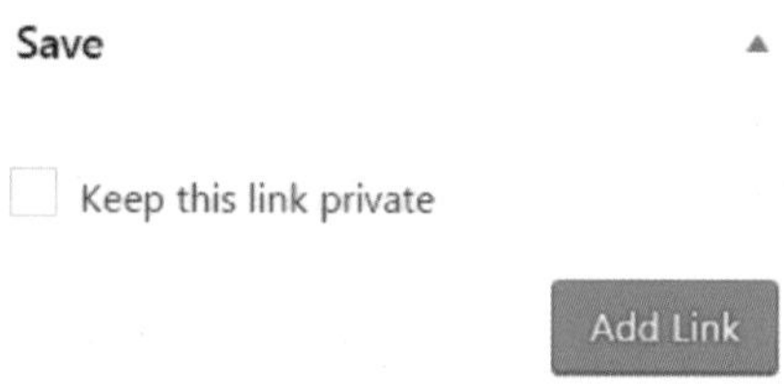

Save

☐ Keep this link private

Add Link

Fig. 6.24 Always save your links.

LINK CATEGORIES

FA Premier League

Fig. 6.25 The screen output.

Finally, don't forget to save your link by clicking **Add Link** and think if there is any point in keeping it private, only available to registered users, but it may be useful if you are offering downloads or other member only information. As a tip create an odd number of links so that the categories are distinguished from each other. WordPress only puts a space between each one. The output from the widget is shown in Figure 6.25 where the larger FA indicates more links of type FA than the much smaller Premier League.

Text

B *I* ☰ ☷ 🔗

Fig. 6.26 The simple editor in the Text widget.

The final *standard* widget is also one of the most useful and versatile as you can put both text and HTML in it. I would leave the HTML side alone as there is a simple editor in the widget as shown in Figure 6.26.

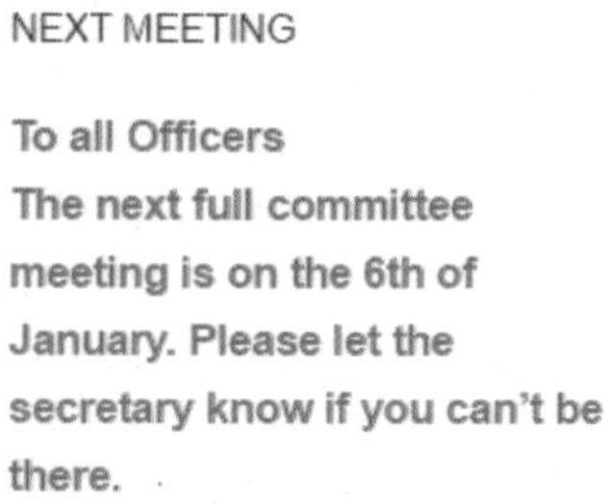

NEXT MEETING

To all Officers
The next full committee meeting is on the 6th of January. Please let the secretary know if you can't be there.

Fig. 6.27 Sample output from Text widget.

This widget is really useful for simple notices and announcements. Figure 6.27 shows a notice as displayed in the Hueman theme.

It is basic but a quick way to add a short message to your website that is easy to update.

Additional Widgets

WordPress is very good but I am sure you could list a few more widgets that would be really useful. A quirk of WordPress is that other widgets are listed as plugins.

Once you find a widget you like, check that it is compatible with the installed version of WordPress and then install it. These additional plugins are listed under **Plugins** where it is activated to be added to the list of available **Widgets** where it is configured. A bit complicated but not too bad once you do it a few times.

Over the next few pages are some of the widgets that WordPress might add in future updates. It is important to have images and graphics on your website as visitors find them interesting. A website with too much text on each page can lead to visitor fatigue.

Image Widget

The widget opens in a simple way by asking you to select an image stored in the media library but then becomes a little more complex. I have split the options into two lots to more easily explain what is going on. Keeping this really simple I have just given the image a title and a caption. The second set of options are about using the image as a visual link to move away from this page to another page in your website or to an external website.

Simple Image

Insert Into Widget

Fig. 6.28 Step 1 is to add an image to the widget.

Expand the widget and click on **Select Image**. Pick one from the **Media Library** or **Upload** a new image and click on the button labelled as **Insert into Widget** (Figure 6.28). Give the Image a Title, use the defaults for all the other options except Size, that may be set to **Full Size**, as shown in Figure 6.29. Change this to **Thumbnail** initially and if that doesn't work then work through the other options with thumb in the name.

Size: Full Size   ▾

Fig. 6.29 The default size in the image widget is Full Size. Start with a smaller image.

Linked Image

The image can be made into a clickable link by putting a URL into the Link box. You might think that you can grab a Link ID from within WordPress, especially if you have already set up links but this will not work. Just add the link using the full URL starting with

Link:

http://www.itv.com

Link ID:

Stay in Window   ▾

Size: Thumbnail

Fig. 6.31 A link set up for a UK TV station.

The result is shown in Figure 6.30. In this example the entries concerning links have not been used. They are blank so the website just has a static image.

BLUE FISH

Fig. 6.30 The output from the static settings .

http://, select the option to **Stay in Window** or **Open New Window** and check that the size has not reverted back to **Full**. See Figure 6.31 for an example. Leave Link ID blank.

Like other widgets only one Image widget is allowed . Finally, don't forget to add a caption that will be displayed under your image.

Map Widget

At some point in its development a website will need a map to show where it is based or to direct people to an event. There are many plugins for Google and not all of them work the way you might expect or look good with a particular theme. You can waste a lot of time trying to bend a widget into shape so if it is not doing what you want after an hour then search for another one or consider a full plugin.

Google Maps Widget

Tired of buggy and slow Google Maps plugins taking hours to setup? With GMW you'll have a perfect map with a thumbnail and lightbox in minutes!

By Web Factory Ltd

Fig. 6.32 The Google Maps Widget is found in the plugin store.

The Google Maps Widget (Figure 6.32) is a good entry level map widget ideal for providing a location to a business, an event or pretty much anything you like provided Google is aware of it or you know the latitude and longitude.

Fig. 6.33 The output is a compact map with a marker pin for the location.

The widget loads up with predefined settings for both its thumbnail map and interactive map. The default location is for New York so select your location or a place you are familiar with to start configuring the map. I picked my local National Trust to produce Figure 6.33.

Hovering over the red pin triggers the invitation to open a larger map. The widget does open a larger map with the underlying website greyed out and to shrink it again the user has to click somewhere on the screen away from the map. The setting that controls this is listed under **Lightbox Features** under the **Interactive** tab as shown in Figure 6.34.

Lightbox Features: [× Close on overlay click]

Fig. 6.34 Look for the Lightbox Features for other options to close the map.

Clicking in the box shows that two other options are available in the PRO version, one of which is to show a **close** button. In the same option box is one to show the map title.

If the widget works randomly with the active theme on your website then you might need to consider upgrading to the paid-for version or using a map plugin.

Configuring the Map Widget

If you are a Google Maps novice then these settings can seem like another language. Use the defaults as these may produce the desired result. There are five tabs and unless you have bought the PRO version you need only concern yourself with the **Thumbnail Map** and the **Interactive Map**.

Thumbnail Map Settings

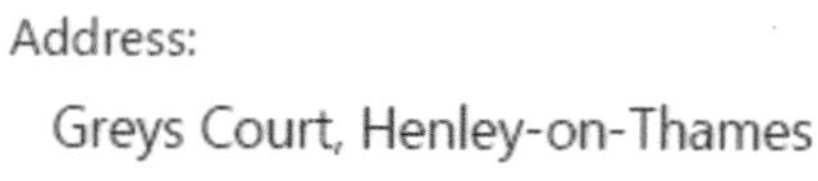

Address:

Greys Court, Henley-on-Thames

Fig. 6.35 Start typing your location and Google will do the rest.

Working from the top down insert a title for your map and it can be whatever you like and then find the location you are looking for by typing in the box. Google is clever and the few words shown in Figure 6.35 found the correct place. Admittedly it is well known. Clicking in the Address box open a help bubble that tells you how to enter a location using latitude and longitude.   If Google returns a location nearby on the map that opens up you can drag a drop the marker pin to the exact location.

Figure 6.36 has the key map settings. The default thumbnail size is 250px by 250px. Click in the box to change that up or down.

Map Size:	250 ⬍ x 250	px
Map Type:	Road (default)	
Color Scheme:	Refreshed by Google	
Zoom Level:	14	

Fig. 6.36 Change the map size if you need to.

Usually **Road** is the one required although there is also **Satellite**, **Hybrid** and **Terrain**. Leave the **Color Scheme** at the Refreshed by Google and I find the zoom level of 14 is good enough. By all means, change these to suit your needs but make a note of the defaults before you do so. The **Marker Pin** settings can be changed to your own preferences and then use the other defaults. Don't forget to Save your changes to activate the new settings.

Interactive Map Settings

There are fewer interactive settings and all the defaults will work without any changes. In fact most of them are disabled and only available in the paid-for version.

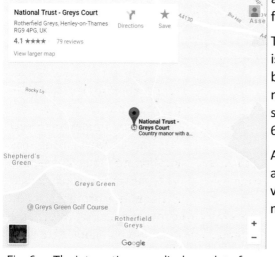

The thumbnail map is lacking in details but the Interactive map looks good as shown in Figure 6.37.

As mentioned, think about the PRO version for much more functionality.

Fig. 6.37 The interactive map displays a lot of details for your potential visitors. If a map is important spend some time trying the various settings.

Login Widget

The Meta widget has the inbuilt limitation that the list of links cannot be changed. On many occasions, all you require is a link for registered users to login.

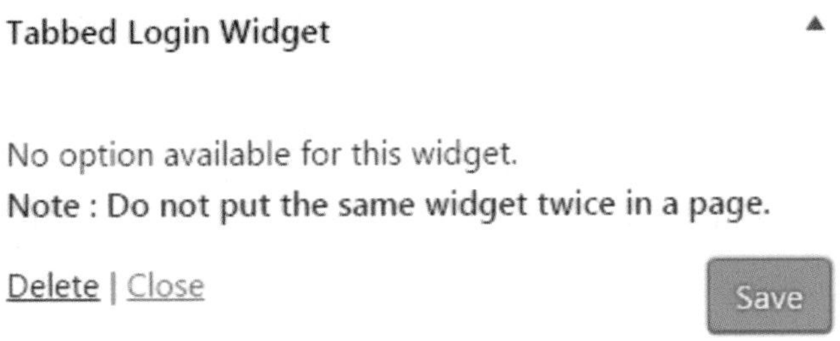

Tabbed Login Widget   ▲

No option available for this widget.
Note : Do not put the same widget twice in a page.

Delete | Close   Save

Fig. 6.38 The widget has no settings. Like most widgets you cannot duplicate it on the same page.

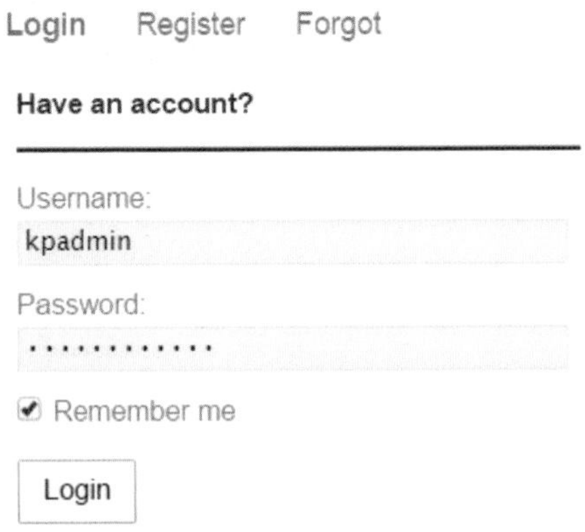

Login   Register   Forgot

Have an account?
_____

Username:
kpadmin

Password:
· · · · · · · · · · · ·

☑ Remember me

Login

Fig. 6.39 The output has all the options a user needs—Login, Register and of course, get a new password.

The Tabbed Login Widget is one of the better alternatives available for WordPress. As before, it is available to download in the plugin area by searching for its full name. Be aware that there are many plugins with similar names so you need to get the name exactly right. There is no configuration and you enable it by moving it to a widget zone. Figure 6.39 shows what a user will see. When you set it up for the first time you may have to logout to see the three tabs. There is the

Register tab for new members and the tab to get a new password sent to you. Standard fare on many websites and essential in these days of multiple passwords.

Moving Widgets About

Widgets are activated differently to plugins . Plugins have a link clearly marked as **Activate** or **De-activate**.

Widgets are activated by dropping from the Available Widgets List onto a widget area or zone like Primary, Secondary or Footer. There is also a parking area for Inactive Widgets.

Unfortunately, WordPress lists all the widgets in the Available list even if they aren't in use. Consider moving the ones you will never use to the Inactive Widgets list. You have to click on the Widget to get WordPress to tell you where it is being used.

To help with configuring widgets click on the Manage with Live Preview button. This simply takes you into the Customization section of the theme configuration.

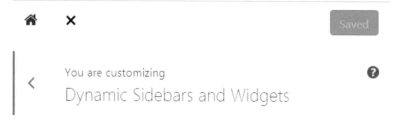

7

WordPress Plugins

A plugin is any additional piece of software that is added to the core WordPress software. Plugins can become widgets and applications after installation. You might need to know this because Plugins are found in their own list, Widgets in the Appearance —> Widgets area and Applications create their own entry in the Dashboard menu.

When you select plugins from the WordPress dashboard side menu a list of all plugins installed on the website, both active and inactive appears on the screen. On a new installation there is Hello Dolly, a bit of WordPress fun and Askimet to block spam. Akismet is inactive by default and it is your choice whether to use it or not.

Akismet

You can safely click on the link to 'Sign up to an Akismet Plan' either using the WordPress account you created by following Appendix 1 or using other credentials. Unfortunately there is nothing really free on the site with the suggested minimum annual donation set at £27.00. For personal use you can pay a nominal amount or nothing at all.

You can block most spam yourself by restricting comments completely or limiting it to registered users that can be blacklisted if they break your guidelines. Go back to the WordPress settings to remind yourself what is possible.

Akismet provides a lot more control by analysing the content of each comment, checking on the number of hyperlinks and any words that you added to the filter list. Akismet is a good tool but is no substitute for a human checking what people are posting.

If you need to take action on spam consider WP-Spamshield, a comprehensive plugin that has many options to block spam in every corner of WordPress or the much simpler Anti-Spam that blocks spam in Comments and has no settings.

Finding Other Plugins

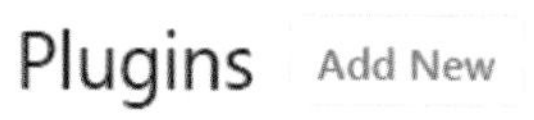

Plugins Add New

Fig. 7.1 Look for this at the top of the plugin list screen.

The easiest way is the click the Add New button on the Plugins screen.

The next screen starts at Featured plugins but if you click on Recommended then around 10,000 are offered up to you.

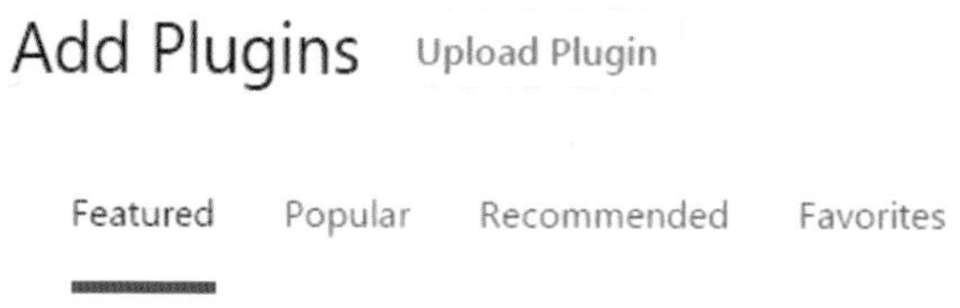

Add Plugins Upload Plugin

Featured   Popular   Recommended   Favorites

Fig. 7.2 Plugins are listed in various ways but a search is the quickest way to find what you are looking for.

Reduce the list by putting some keywords into the search box. Not all plugins are listed on WordPress.org and many more are registered on developer websites.

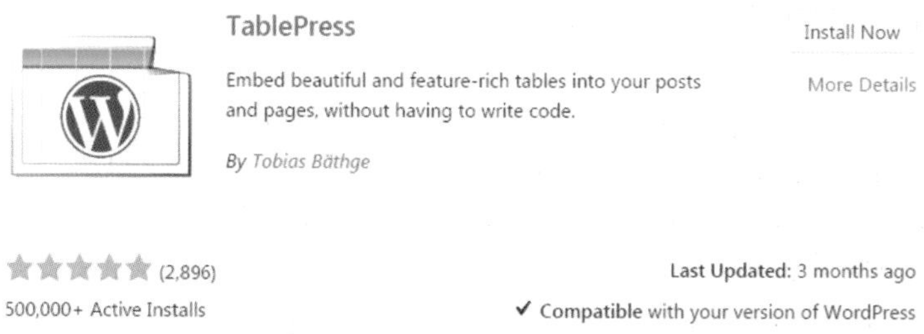

TablePress   Install Now

Embed beautiful and feature-rich tables into your posts   More Details
and pages, without having to write code.

By Tobias Bäthge

★★★★★ (2,896)   Last Updated: 3 months ago

500,000+ Active Installs   ✓ Compatible with your version of WordPress

Fig. 7.3 A typical plugin listing in WordPress.

The listing provides some valuable information on each Plugin. Under the plugin name is a short description of what it does.

Check how many stars the plugin has received, (see Figure 7.3) and by how many users , the number in brackets. Always check that the plugin is compatible with the installed version of WordPress and ,if not, do not use it. It may work but if there are any issues then you will spend a lot of time working out ways round the problems.

Also note when the last update happened and if it is over 6 months then it is either very stable and simple plugin or the developer has moved on. Equally, frequent updates can be a sign of an unstable product. It is impossible to cover everything that you might want to add to a website. The next few pages cover the most common things a small organisation might need.

Maps

If maps are mentioned then Google Maps is the name that usually crops up. There are a handful of plugins for other providers like Bing but most developers stay with Google. Putting the keywords in returns nearly 1,200 possible plugins based on Goggle Maps.

Keyword ▾   Google Maps

Fig. 7.4 A simple search narrows the list of possible plugins.

For a really simple location map to help visitors to your website with directions use a search like 'Google Map'. For a map with more information consider using the Map widget covered in Chapter 6.

Google Map

Simple, light-weight and non-bloated WordPress Google Map Plugin.

By Ankur Kumar

Ank Google Map

Fig. 7.5 Google Map is one of the easier to use plugins.

Google is very protective of its map technology and every map user needs to register with Google to get an API key. API stands for Application Programming Interface, the gateway to the software that will accept a range of commands . It is essential to do this because the plugin will not work without it.

The easiest way to do this is to select your plugin and the one that I have had success with is Google Map as shown in Figure 7.5.

Click on Install button found next to the icon shown on page 130 and when the button changes to Activate click on that. Open the list of plugins installed by clicking on the Plugins menu on the WordPress dashboard to find the entry for Google Map.

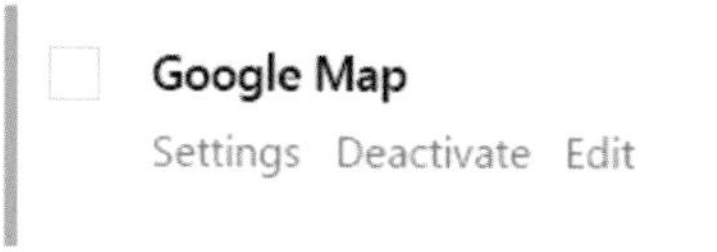

Google Map

Settings   Deactivate   Edit

Fig. 7.6 The plugin list has links to activate and deactivate plugins.

Click on the Settings link to find out how to configure it. The plugin won't work properly (see Figure 7.7) without a valid Google API key and will come up with a rather obscure technical error.

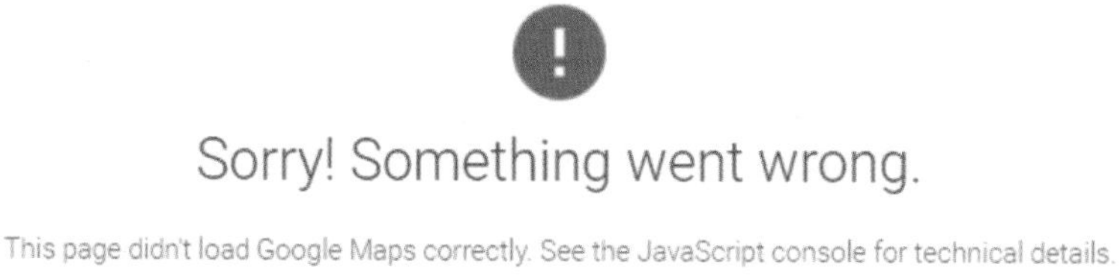

Sorry! Something went wrong.

This page didn't load Google Maps correctly. See the JavaScript console for technical details.

Fig. 7.7 The error from Google is dramatic but not serious.

Google Map (v2.5.0)

General   Location   Marker   Info Window

API Key   AIzaSyB3he9SSWeblYpk ❓

Fig. 7.8 The Google Map settings with the API entry box.

To obtain an API, click on the blue question mark above the entry box (Figure 7.8). The API is free for most web sites so ignore Google's invitation to sign up to paid-for plans. If you don't have a Google account, a Gmail login will suffice, then you will need to acquire a free one. Do a Google search to find the place to apply for an account and then a second search to sign up for the API map key.

The API process is straightforward and Google will flag up any errors. The API is issued on a per website basis so do always get a new one. The final stage is to give your project a name, one of your own or one of the ones suggested by Google that usually ends up being My Project and the API key will be produced. Remember to copy it off the screen and then paste it into the API field in the Google Map plugin.

Setting up the Google Map plugin

The Google Map plugin installs its control panel in the Settings menu on the WordPress dashboard. The settings has four tabs as shown in Figure 7.10. Work through the tabs one by one.

Fig. 7.9 The plugin has its own menu entry on the dashboard.

At this stage, on the General tab, accept all the suggested defaults and enter the API key that Google issued. Then, on the Location tab use the search field in the map section at the bottom labelled **Set Location**.

General	Location	Marker	Info Window

Fig. 7.10 the Google Map plugin tabs in settings.

Type in the name of the location adding more details until the one you want appears in the list.

Fig. 7.11 Starting typing to find your location.

You can use the latitude and longitude if you wish but you need to use the decimal format shown in Figure 7.12.

Latitude   51.54520000000001

Longitude   -0.9515099999999848

Fig. 7.12 You can use a standard geographic system if you want.

You cannot get the level of precision achieved by Google. Use latitude and longitude to two decimal points and then move the marker pin on the map. On the **Marker** and **Info Windows** tab start with the defaults and change the options one at a time until you get the effect you want.

Remember, the Google Map plugin will not display a map unless you have an API key from Google. There are many other plugins available but are generally more complicated to set up than this one. If you need more features then it is a process of installing a plugin, using it and moving on if necessary.

Using the Google Map plugin

The plugin uses a WordPress coding feature called a shortcode to insert the map information set up in the plugin. The shortcode can then be used in a post or page to produce a map. The shortcode can be used in more than one post or page.

Plugin. Short code : [ank_google_map]

Fig. 7.13 This is the code that creates the map. Many WordPress codes are shown inside square brackets in the editor.

A small flaw with this plugin is that the shortcode is not displayed when you set up the location. The code is displayed in the plugin section as shown in Figure 7.13.

Figure 7.14 shows the shortcode included in a post aimed at directing visitors to a venue. The plugin does not support multiple codes so you can only set up one location at a time.

Using the plugin with a post lets you add a lot more information about directions, parking and whatever else your visitors need to know. The map or the canvas will fill the whole width of the post or page and might just cause problems on mobile devices.

If it does, use the % setting to make it responsive and alter some or all of the other Canvas options until in looks right. The Canvas options are found in the General tab (Figure 7.10).

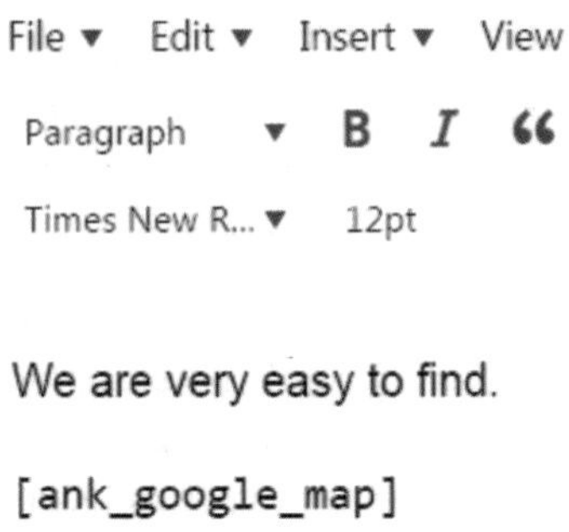
File ▾ Edit ▾ Insert ▾ View
Paragraph ▾ B I “
Times New R... ▾ 12pt
We are very easy to find.
[ank_google_map]

Fig. 7.14 The shortcode in a post.

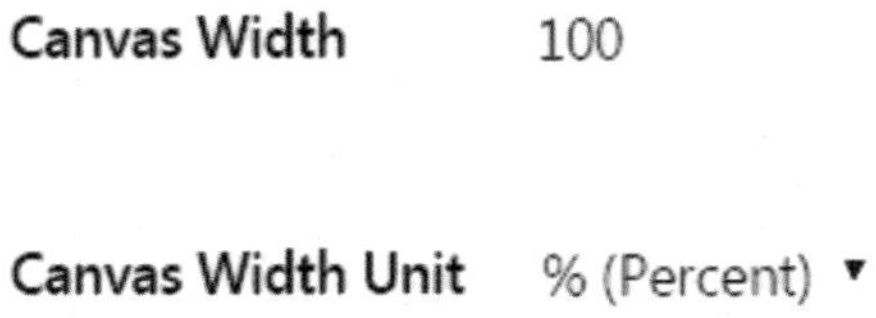
Canvas Width 100
Canvas Width Unit % (Percent) ▾

Fig. 7.15 Some of the canvas options. Using % makes the map responsive, suitable for mobile devices.

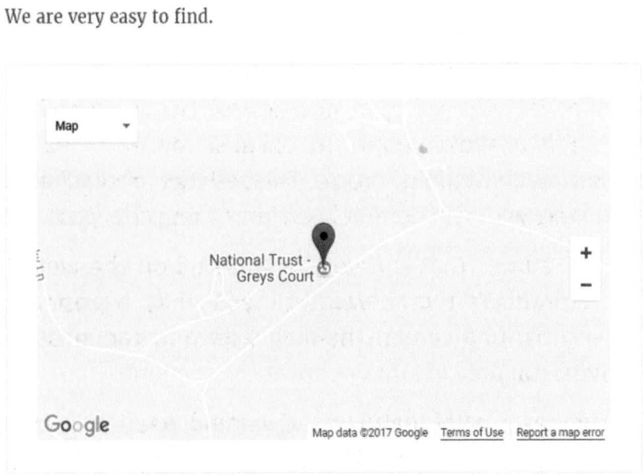
We are very easy to find.
Map
National Trust - Greys Court
+
−
Google
Map data ©2017 Google
Terms of Use
Report a map error

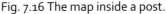

Fig. 7.16 The map inside a post.

Newsletters

There are 900 hits when you search for a plugin to make a newsletter. MailPoet tops many reviews of the top newsletter makers.

MailPoet Newsletters

Send newsletters post notifications or autoresponders from WordPress easily, and beautifully. Start to capture subscribers with our widget now.

By MailPoet

Fig. 7.17 A highly rated newsletter plugin.

After installing it a new entry will appear in the dashboard but it may take a minute or two.

Fig. 7.18 MailPoet puts a menu on the dashboard.

Mailpoet has a welcome screen with an introductory video and where you can sign up for their newsletter.

Mailpoet teaches you how to make a newsletter by getting you to edit the one included in the software. The editor is separate to the WordPress one and works on a drag and drop basis. Spend some time on this to create professional newsletters that people will love to read.

Open the **Settings** menu to view the six tabs that let you set up a newsletter that is compliant with requirements to allow people to unsubscribe and clearly show where the e-mail is coming from. The settings are well explained and again start with the defaults before making changes.

MailPoet assumes that everyone registered on the website will be a subscriber. You may want to edit that by opening the **Subscribers** menu to create mailing lists and move users into them as necessary.

The plugin has a lot of features and you will need to spend some time learning how to use it. There is also a simple Widget, titled

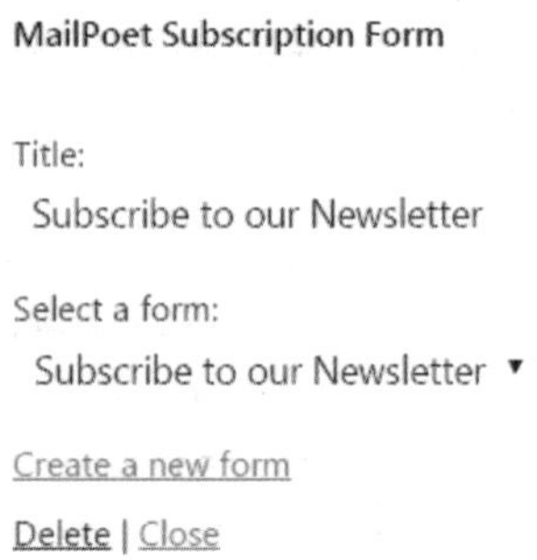

MailPoet Subscription Form

Title:
Subscribe to our Newsletter

Select a form:
Subscribe to our Newsletter ▼

Create a new form

Delete | Close

Fig. 7.19 The MailPoet widget . Set it up in the Widget submenu on the Appearance menu on the dashboard.

the **MailPoet Subscription Form**, that can be used to capture subscribers and visitors just visiting the website. The setup for the widget is shown in Figure 7.19 and the registration box is shown in Figure 7.20.

There is a section in the Mailpoet settings tab to include an option to sign up for a newsletter subscription as part of the registering process. This option is linked to the general WordPress Settings to let anyone register on the website. Check that setting in WordPress itself if you have any problems. Once you tick the box other options appear including one to subscribe to more than one of your newsletters.

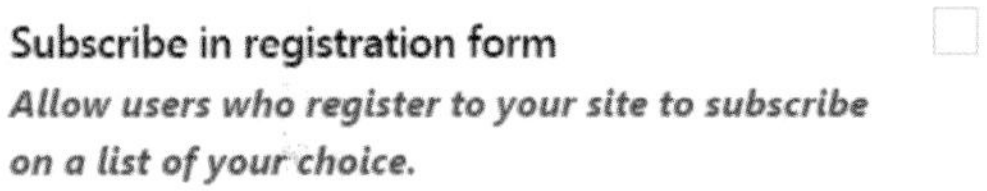

Subscribe in registration form

Allow users who register to your site to subscribe on a list of your choice.

Fig. 7.20 The registration setting.

Using MailPoet

The plugin ships with one basic theme that also serves as a short tutorial on how to use the software. Several other themes (Figure 7.21) are available to download and one of them might be a better fit for your activities.

Content   Images   Styles   **Themes**

Add more themes

Fig. 7.21 MailPoet has a number of themes for you to download.

Above the installed themes icons is a tabbed section that

what you send is just awesome !

Step 1: hey, click on this text!

To edit, simply click on this block of text.

Step 2: play with this image

Position your mouse over the image to the left.

Fig. 7.22 The start of the tutorial. Its approach looks a little childish but stick with it.

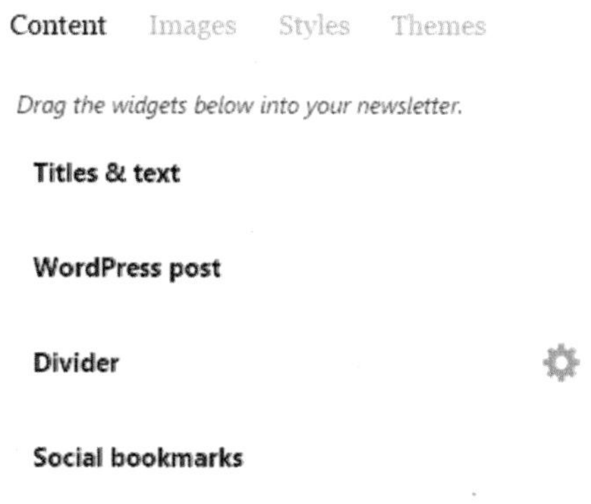

Content   Images   Styles   Themes

Drag the widgets below into your newsletter.

Titles & text

WordPress post

Divider

Social bookmarks

Fig. 7.23 The Content tab is where you can access your posts for inclusion in your newsletter.

accesses content and images already stored in the database.

The tutorial must be worked through in steps that show you how to edit content, change images and drop in posts from the blog (Figure 7.22).

When you are finished adding content delete the step-by-step instructions by highlighting them or hovering over them and pressing delete or tapping/clicking on the X button. You will find all this out by working with the plugin. It is worth the effort as the end result is good.

To insert links to posts and pages click on the Content tab (Figure 7.23) , **WordPress post** and then drag the **post** to the newsletter and drop it when an area is highlighted with a message saying ' **Insert New Block Here**'.

Images can be selected from WordPress or uploaded from your device and a thumbnail is added to the sidebar.

The final step invites you to change the Footer but before you click on the **Settings** button remember to save your changes or they will be lost. The default settings should be good enough for most newsletters. Simply delete this section to finish your first newsletter.

Now, you can send a preview of the newsletter to an e-mail address to see how it will look.

Fig. 7.24 Save your changes and send a review copy to yourself to check what it will look like in reality.

Targeting Subscribers

Click on Next Step (Figure 7.24) to complete the process. Edit the Subject Line to give the newsletter a name. Next choose who is going to receive it. MailPoet assumes that the newsletter is going to everyone registered on the system.

Fig. 7.25 You can send your newsletter to one or more lists .

If this is not the case then you will need to create another list and add subscribers manually.

You need to select at least one list before you press the Send button. If there are no lists then create one by clicking on Add List in the Mailpoet Subscribers menu item on the WordPress dashboard.

A nice feature is that MailPoet delays sending for about 10 minutes, allowing you to delay the newsletters going out.

Adding a List

Lists and Subscribers   Add Subscriber   Add List   Edit Lists

Fig. 7.26 Create as many lists as you need using the Subscribers
        menu.

Creating your own list, say of all the society's officers is easy to do. Click on the Subscribers link in the MailPoet menu to access all the lists available. Click on Edit Lists, hover over the list and then on View Subscribers. On the top menu bar will be an option to Add Subscriber and give them an initial status. Once you find your way around it is all very easy to do.

Settings

MailPoet has a lot of settings and you shouldn't need to change any of them. If e-mails are not going out the Send With tab has a button to send a test e-mail to a specified address.

 On the Advanced tab you might want to add a Bounce E-Mail address to detect any subscribers who might have changed their e-mail provider. Some people do that quite frequently.

The Newsletter

As an e-mail   in an inbox, part of which is shown in Fig. 7.27, the first draft probably would benefit from a little more work, so that the content is neatly formatted and looks professional.

 At the bottom of the e-mail are links to unsubscribe, very important as a newsletter sender and an option to edit the recipients subscription if there are other newsletters available. See Figure 7.28.

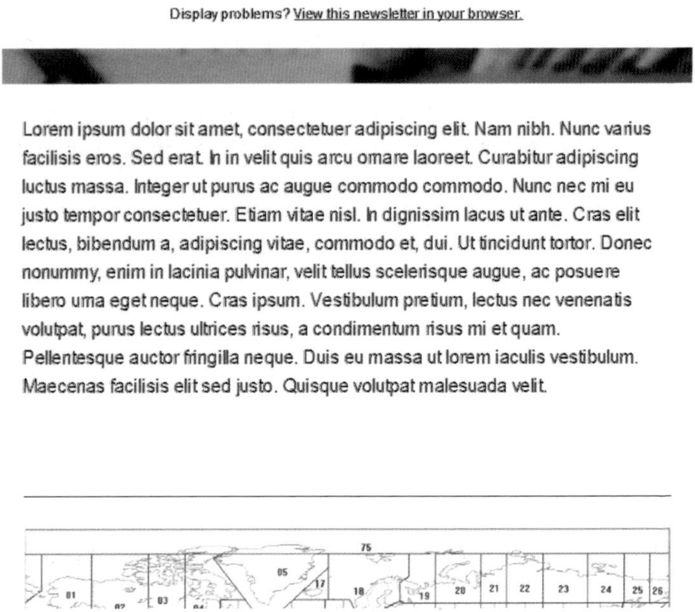

Display problems? View this newsletter in your browser.

Lorem ipsum dolor sit amet, consectetuer adipiscing elit. Nam nibh. Nunc varius facilisis eros. Sed erat. In in velit quis arcu ornare laoreet. Curabitur adipiscing luctus massa. Integer ut purus ac augue commodo commodo. Nunc nec mi eu justo tempor consectetuer. Etiam vitae nisl. In dignissim lacus ut ante. Cras elit lectus, bibendum a, adipiscing vitae, commodo et, dui. Ut tincidunt tortor. Donec nonummy, enim in lacinia pulvinar, velit tellus scelerisque augue, ac posuere libero urna eget neque. Cras ipsum. Vestibulum pretium, lectus nec venenatis volutpat, purus lectus ultrices risus, a condimentum risus mi et quam. Pellentesque auctor fringilla neque. Duis eu massa ut lorem iaculis vestibulum. Maecenas facilisis elit sed justo. Quisque volutpat malesuada velit.

Fig. 7.27 A screengrab of the first draft of the newsletter. There is a header, a post and then an image. In between is one of the dividers , a horizontal line, that are available into MailPoet.

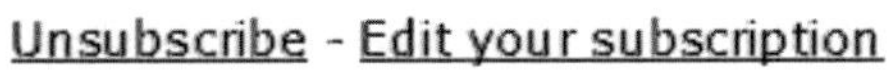

Unsubscribe - Edit your subscription

Fig. 7.28 At the bottom of the newsletter are links to let your subscribers opt out of the newsletter list and to edit their subscription. Almost a legal requirement these days.

Contact Forms

In this section I will introduce you to two contact forms. The first one installs as another widget. You never really know if you have a plugin or a widget until you install the add-on. There are many other contact forms available to try out if these recommendations don't meet your needs.

Simple Contact Form

Very Simple Contact Form

This is a very simple contact form. Use shortcode [contact] to display form on page or use the widget.

By Guido van der Leest

Fig. 7.29 Another add-on that can be a plugin or a widget.

A search for 'Simple Contact Form' should return the widget shown in Figure 7.29. As it is a widget it will be found on the dashboard under **Appearance —> Widgets**. The widget has two options, shown in Figure 7.30, its name and whether you want to change any attributes.

You don't have to worry about setting attributes as the widget produces a nice output on the web page. The contact messages are sent to the administrator's e-mail address.

Very Simple Contact Form: Contact Us

Title:
Contact Us

Information:

Fig. 7.30 The widget is easy to set up.

The widget has a simple anti-spam feature that will work well enough on most websites.

You can change the defaults, such

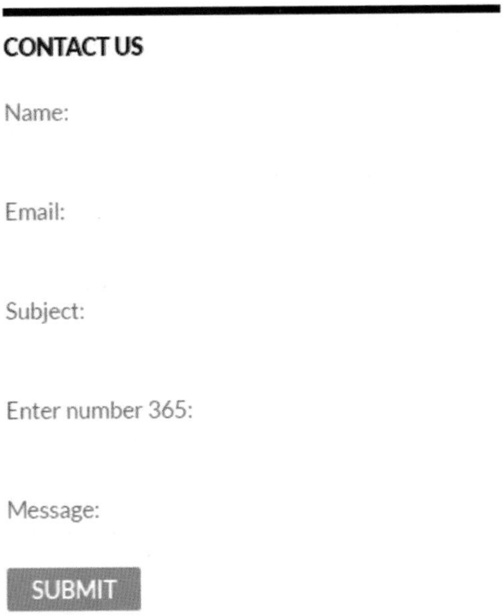

CONTACT US

Name:

Email:

Subject:

Enter number 365:

Message:

SUBMIT

Fig. 7.31 The Widget's output. It can be positioned in any of the widget locations.

as the label names, and the attributes, by following the help guide found by clicking on the link in the widget page. The link is titled as follows: **Info about attributes.**

Study the guide closely, and then enter the following to change the label 'Name' to 'Your Name' or whatever you want.

[contact label_name="Your Name"] and Save the widget.

If you find that the second square bracket appears on the screen then omit it. You can change all of the labels but you can't add new ones. The following changed both the name and e-mail labels as shown in Figure 7.32.

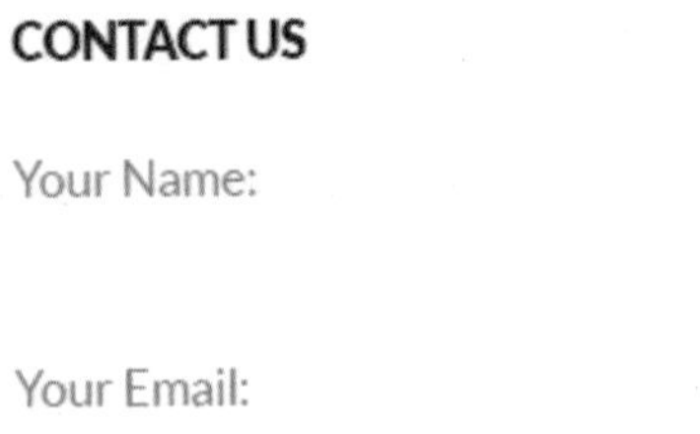

CONTACT US

Your Name:

Your Email:

[contact   label_name   ="Your Name"   label_email   ="Your Email"

You can change the other labels in the same way to make a customised contact form.

Fig. 7.32 A modified contact form.

Storing the contact messages in the database

It is possible to store the contact messages in the database if you want. It involves another plugin but this one is not in the WordPress repository. The developer has stored it in another well-known developers' web-based store called GitHub. The help pages provide the link. There is a WordPress link but the plugin is not listed.

Downloads

📄 contact-form-7-to-database-extension-2.10.32.zip

Fig. 7.33 The link to the external plugin.

Clicking on the .zip file shown in Figure 7.33 should download it into your Downloads folder. WordPress handles .zip files and there is no need to do anything other than upload it to the system. Don't unzip or extract the files to your device as this makes the process more complicated.

Add Plugins   Upload Plugin

Fig. 7.34 This is where you upload a plugin from your device.

Installing a Plugin from an External File

You only need to do this on a few occasions but it is worth knowing the procedure. On the WordPress dashboard click on the **Plugins** menu, select **Add New**, and then at the top of the screen click on the **Upload Plugin** button (Fig. 7.34). Next click on the **Choose File** button, that will open the File Manager on your device, and now search for the file that you just downloaded. Next, click on the **Install Now** button to begin the upload from your device to the server and the installation of the plugin on the WordPress system.

Choose file contact-form-...-2.10.32.zip   Install Now

Fig. 7.35 Once you have the correct file click on Install Now and WordPress finishes the job for you.

Unpacking the package...

Installing the plugin...

Plugin installed successfully.

[Activate Plugin]   Return to Plugin Installer

Fig. 7.36 Wait for the Activate Plugin
button to appear on your screen.

If all goes well, and it usually does, you will see a progress guide and another button to **Activate Plugin**. Go ahead and do that.

The plugin will be listed with the others but this plugin adds its own menu to the dashboard (Figure 7.37).

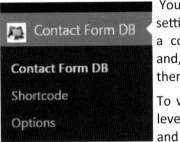

Fig. 7.37 A new menu entry
installs on the dashboard.

You don't need to configure any settings or options. To test it out, send a contact message from the website and, in addition to the copy via email, there is also a copy in the database.

To view the messages click on the top level of the menu, the blue background and then check the database is linked to

Very Simple Contact Form ▾

Fig. 7.38 CFDB connect.

the Very Simple Contact Form. If not, then select it. The database should list the message you just sent. Clicking on the entry gives a formatted summary of the message with the option to delete it.

Show **All** ▾ **entries**

Delete ☐	Submitted
☼	☼
☐	2017-05-22 15:11:15 +00:00

Showing 1 to 1 of 1 entries

Fig. 7.39 A sample entry in the database.

Having a database of messages may be much more than you need but having an audit trail can be useful for follow-up queries of all sorts.

More Versatile Contact Forms

If your business activity is all about building up a list of contacts then you might need a more configurable form. If spam e-mail becomes a problem you might need to add better anti-spam defences.

Contact Form 7

Contact forms can be good and bad. Good in that visitors to the website have a way to get in touch and potentially bad by attracting spammers to it, so wasting time and possibly installing malware on your website.

Contact Form 7

Just another contact form plugin. Simple but flexible.

By Takayuki Miyoshi

Fig. 7.40 Look for this entry in the WordPress plugin repository.

Flamingo

A trustworthy message storage plugin for Contact Form 7.

By Takayuki Miyoshi

Fig. 7.41 The associated plugin.

You are now getting familiar with the plugin routine of installing , activing and then looking either for a settings link in the plugin list or an additional menu item in the dashboard or possibly a widget.

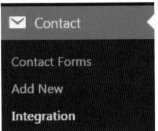

Fig. 7.42 Look for this addition to the dashboard.

Contact Form 7 has a settings link and two helpful messages appear on the dashboard. **Akismet** has been covered already and we will briefly look at the other products suggested by this developer.

Flamingo

Flamingo (Fig. 7.41) has its own menu on the dashboard that is simply the list of known users on the system in an Address Book and a second list of the inbound messages.

reCAPTCHA

You will have encountered this on the internet but probably never knew the name of the technology. This is where you have to demonstrate that you are a human and not a robot belonging to a spammer. Google bought this technology and you need to get a key to link your website to the anti-spam system. This is a similar process to acquiring an API key for Google maps.

There is a **Contact** menu (Figure 7.42) in the dashboard and opening the **Integration** link shows you how to get a key.

Click on the **google.com/recpatcha** link and follow the instructions to register your domain. Open a new tab in your browser at this point as it will make it easier to copy the two keys generated by the process before pasting them into the boxes on the WordPress dashboard. If all goes well then a confirmation will appear on your WordPress admin screen.

Creating a Contact Form

Now click on Contact Forms menu item (Figure 7.42) to open the list of forms and **duplicate** the sample contact form so that you can always refer back to it and keep it as a guide to troubleshooting

The plugin has its own editor with a list of blocks that can be inserted into your contact form. Position your cursor where you would like a block to appear. Some blocks, text, email and textarea are in the sample form and they give you a good idea how this works. Having set up the anti-spam feature I simply added the recaptcha feature to my form that I renamed Contact Us. All the other options in the three other tabs don't need changing at this stage.

SAVE your form and this message will appear with a shortcode (Figure 7.43) to insert into a post or a page.

Contact Us

Copy this shortcode and paste it into your post, page, or text widget content:

`[contact-form-7 id="128" title="Contact Us"]`

Fig. 7.43 The plugin produces some text (highlighted) that you can copy and paste into a page or post to be included in a menu.

To test out your form create a new post, also called Contact Us. Copy and Paste the shortcode produced by the plugin (Figure 7.43). It will look like **[contact-form-7 id="128" title="Contact Us"]** and **Publish** your post.

Help us defeat spam

You will have to add the post to a menu to get it to appear on your website. Anti-spam features give people a little more confidence to send a message as they know you are being security minded.

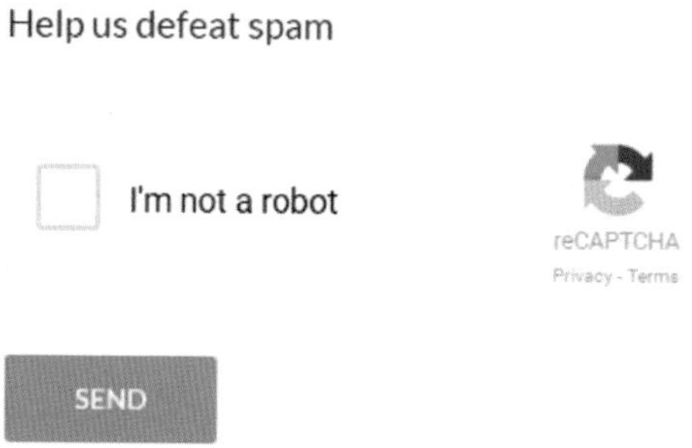

Fig. 7.44 A message asking users to confirm that they are human.

How it was done

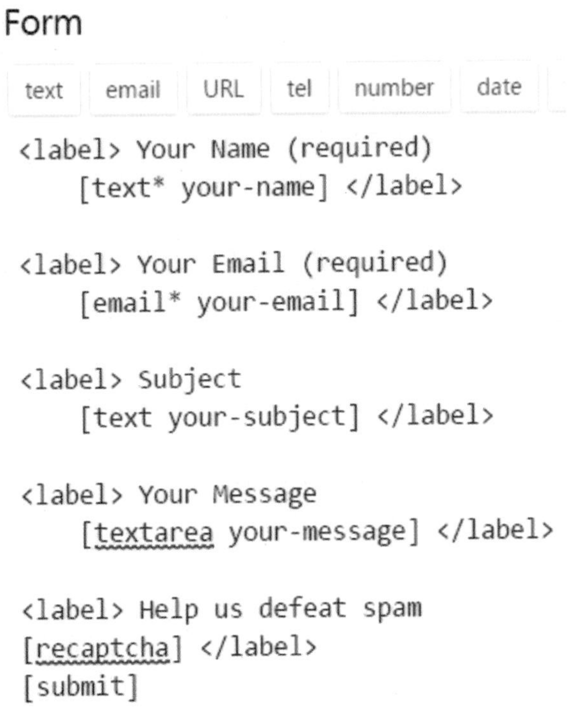

Form

| text | email | URL | tel | number | date |

```
<label> Your Name (required)
     [text* your-name] </label>

<label> Your Email (required)
     [email* your-email] </label>

<label> Subject
     [text your-subject] </label>

<label> Your Message
     [textarea your-message] </label>

<label> Help us defeat spam
[recaptcha] </label>
[submit]
```

Fig. 7.45 This is the markup, it is not strictly code, used to produce the form. Most of it was supplied by the developer.

Here is the markup (Figure 7.45) used to generate this form. The only additional line added to the sample form is the one to place the anti-spam device onto the website. That line starts with **[recaptcha]**.

I like this plugin but it is not that robust. You need to keep your forms as simple as possible otherwise the plugin inserts extra lines and whitespace where you don't want them.

Images

Images make a website more interesting and help retain visitors' attention. Long passages of text, although sometimes necessary are hard to read.

  We have seen how to add images to posts and pages as well as a single image in a sidebar using a widget. There are times when a portfolio or slideshow of images are a vital addition to your website. People love to look through photos of events, possibly a catalogue of your own work or a series of pictures of a very picturesque place. As always there are several hundred plugins available to add images but a simple solution is often the best.

Simple Gallery

Simple Gallery

Lightbox Gallery plugin is allow users to view larger versions of images, simple slide shows...

By Weblizar

Fig. 7.46 Look for this plugin in the repository.

Fig. 7.47 The menu.

Follow the usual sequence to install and activate the plugin and a new menu item, Lightbox Gallery, appears on the dashboard menu(Fig. 7.47).

Step one is to **Add Lightbox Gallery**, give it a title and then add some images to it. This is a straight-forward process. The images need to be either in or uploaded to the Media Library. The selected images are displayed for you to add a caption to each one or simply discard it.

Below the images is a list of options for the gallery and each image. There are too many to go through here and I would encourage you to start with the defaults and then change some options to see what effect they will have. To add the gallery to a page or post copy the shortcode shown on the right hand side. It will be different for each gallery that you create. Don't forget to **Publish** your gallery otherwise all your work will be lost. Now let's add that code to a new page .

Fig. 7.48 You have to add images to your gallery from the media library.

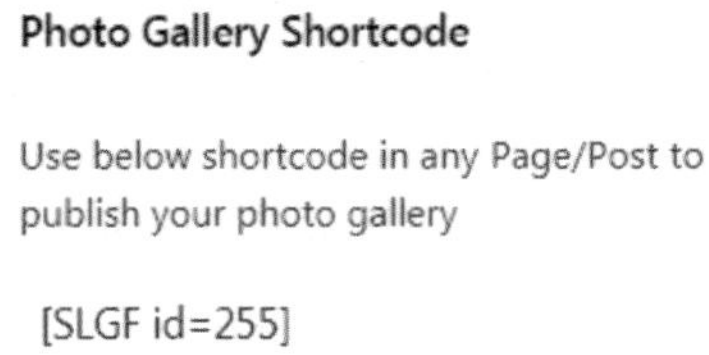

Photo Gallery Shortcode

Use below shortcode in any Page/Post to publish your photo gallery

[SLGF id=255]

Fig. 7.49 Gallery Shortcode.

The plugin has added a helpful button to the page and post editor to add a photo gallery. You have two options. Click on the button and choose your gallery as shown in Figure 7.50 or manually insert the code if you have made a record of it.

Add New Page

Fascinating Fish

As shown in Figure 7.51 click on the button to insert the gallery shortcode into a post. The shortcode text should look like **[SLGF id=123].**

Add Media   Simple Lightbox Gallery Shortcode

File ▼   Edit ▼   Insert ▼   View ▼   Format ▼   Table ▼

Fig. 7.50 Create a new page for your gallery. Note that Lightbox has a button to add in a code.

Next add this post to a menu of your choice and update

Select Lightbox Gallery to insert into post

Select Lightbox Gallery to insert into post

Fish of the Caribbean ▾ | Insert Gallery Shortcode

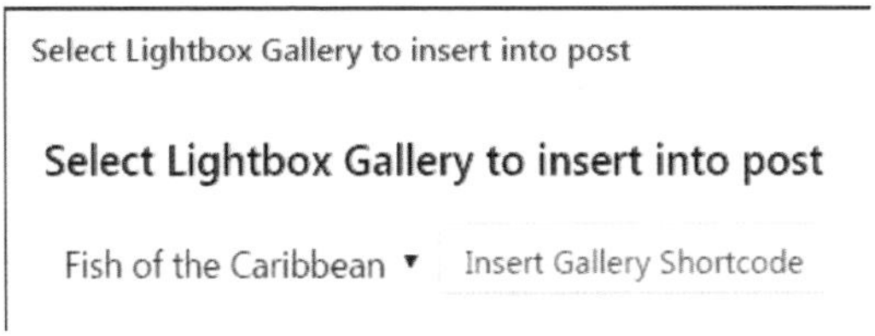

Fig. 7.51 A simple click or tap inserts your gallery into your post.

your menu to display it on your website.

Once the page or post has loaded with a gallery of thumbnail images just hover over one of the thumbnails to see the effect.

Next click on an image to expand it and right at the bottom will be a simple scrolling feature as well as an X to click to get back to the page.

The same gallery can be added to other pages via the same shortcode.

If the layout is not as you want then change some of the options. If you change too many things and it all gets in a mess simply create a new gallery to check the default settings and fix your broken one.

FASCINATING FISH

The fish in the Caribbean are so varied and highly coloured. Here are some I caught on camera.

Fish of the Caribbean

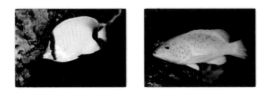

Fig. 7.52 A simple page with your image gallery.

Document Downloads

Clubs and societies usually have documents of various kinds for people to view or download and print off.

A very quick way to do this is to upload your documents to the media library and then click on **Add Media** to add them to a page or post as a link. For example, create a new page called

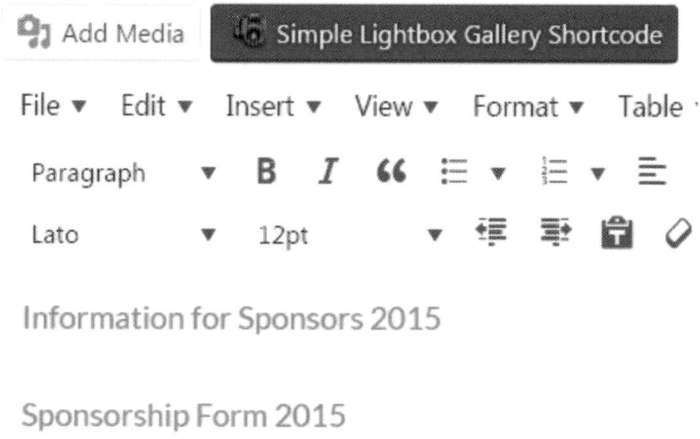

Fig. 7.53 A page with links to your documents.

Membership and add a link to a document that is either in the **Media Library** or added to it using Upload File. Add some **link text** to the URL and **Publish** the document as shown in Figure 7.53.

WordPress creates an internal link to the document and you can add other explanatory text before and after the link. For a handful of documents this is a simple but effective way to make the documents available on the website.

The visitor to your website clicks on a link and their browser will download and open the document in its native format if it supports the format. Documents in the PDF format rarely cause a problem, whereas Microsoft formats will simply result in a file being added to the Downloads folder.

Documents can be restricted to registered users of the website by making the page or post hosting the links **private** rather than **public.** If you want to know how many times a document has been viewed or downloaded there is no way of gathering that information.

Download Monitor

Download Monitor is a plugin for uploading and managing downloads, tracking downloads, and displaying links.

By Never5

Fig. 7.54 Look for Download Monitor in the repository.

Download Monitor

All Downloads

Add New

Categories

Tags

Logs

Settings

Extensions

Fig. 7.55 The new menu on the dashboard.

This is a nice plugin that has a number of features.   By now you are used to the sequence. Once installed look at the Dashboard menu and click on Downloads.

Start with **All Downloads** that opens a **new screen** and then **+ADD file**. A bit like the Gallery Plugin, you **Upload** files from WordPress into the Download Monitor.   Next, click on **Add Media** and then select your file from the library or upload a new one.   Don't worry that this screen says **Insert into Post**, the file is being added to the Downloads database. Publish the document to save your work and note the shortcode to access the document. Go back to All Downloads and your new document should be in the list. Now open the page called Membership that you just created and replace one of the links with the shortcode and Publish it to update it. Do this by clicking on the **Insert Download** button, select your download using the radio buttons and then click on the **Insert Shortcode** button (Fig. 7.56).

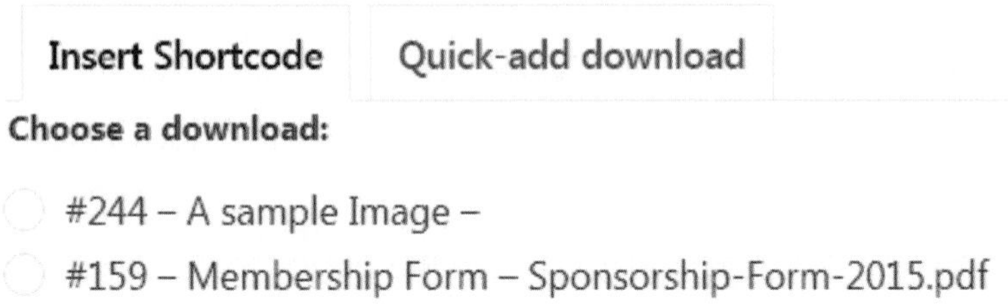
Insert Shortcode
Quick-add download
Choose a download:
#244 – A sample Image –
#159 – Membership Form – Sponsorship-Form-2015.pdf

Fig. 7.56 Pick your download from the list.

This is a simple download link and the browser will not try to open the document with any installed software on the device. The format of the download link may look a bit ragged but you can improve it.

Download "Membership Form"
Sponsorship-Form-2015.pdf - Downloaded 3 times - 252 KB

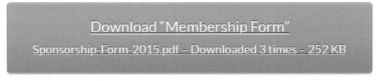

Fig. 7.57 A CSS styled button .

In the **Settings** you can change the formatting of the link by selecting another template under the **General** tab. Choose the second option of a CSS styled button to get a more attractive download link (see the result in Figure 7.57). The plugin has other controls to restrict access to logged in users as well as logging download activity.

The plugin lets you create **Categories** and **Tags** just for downloads and the **Logs** list information on who downloaded which document. The developer has created a suite of paid-for **Extensions** that might be of interest.

8

WordPress Menus

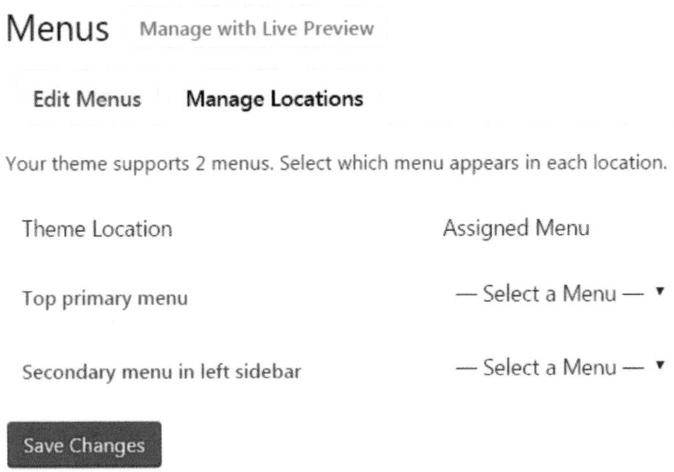

Menus   Manage with Live Preview

Edit Menus   **Manage Locations**

Your theme supports 2 menus. Select which menu appears in each location.

Theme Location	Assigned Menu
Top primary menu	— Select a Menu — ▾
Secondary menu in left sidebar	— Select a Menu — ▾

Save Changes

Fig. 8.1 Managing your menus.

It is very important to understand and master WordPress menus as they provide access to your pages and posts. We have seen the number of menus is governed by the theme where it is common to have just two locations in which to enable a menu.

To recap, you can check the available positions for menus by going to the **Appearance** menu on the dashboard and opening the link to **Menus** (Figure 8.1).

First of all ,open the **Manage Locations** tab and check how many positions you have. When you do this for the first time you will probably find that no menus are assigned even though the website clearly has a menu in each position.

WordPress is being helpful here and assigned default menus to each location. The options are duplicated in the **Customize** theme link. The Twenty Fourteen series of themes has just two positions that is usually adequate. If you need more than you will have to search for a new theme and explore its features. I have mentioned the Hueman theme a few times and that theme has three locations adding a location just above the footer area.

Select a menu to edit: Membership (Topbar) ▾   Select   or create a new menu.

Fig. 8.2 Click on Create New Menu.

Switching back to the **Menus** tab click on create a new menu, give it a name (Membership) and click on **Create New Menu**.

Menu Name   Membership

Menu Structure

Add menu items from the column on the left.

Menu Settings

Auto add pages   Automatically add new top-level pages to this menu

Display location   ☐ Top primary menu (Currently set to: Header1)
☐ Secondary menu in left sidebar (Currently set to: Header)

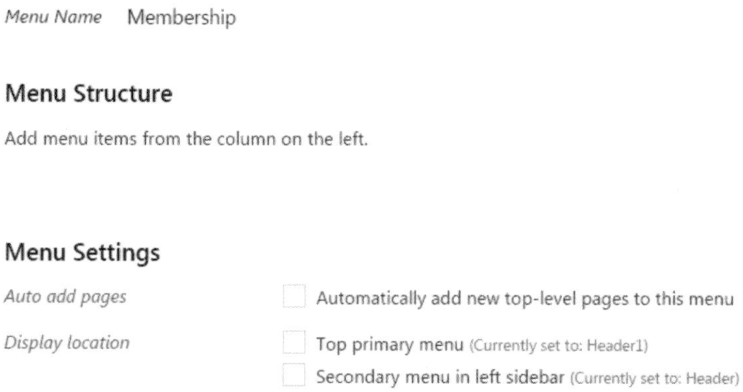

Fig. 8.3 The main menu settings.

Now there are options for Menu Structure, adding menu items, and Menu Settings as shown in Figure 8.3. I rarely opt to **automatically add new top level pages** as it can cause your menus to overflow their locations and affect the images and text on your web pages.

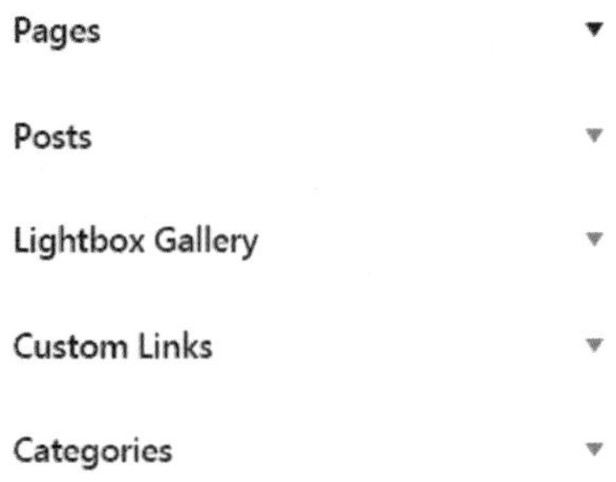

In WordPress you can't have two menus in the same display location and a new menu will displace the old one. I would certainly welcome it if WordPress stacked the two menus on top of one another. The menus are versatile and pages, posts and galleries can be added to them. Note that you can create custom links to other websites as well as whole categories (Figure 8.4).

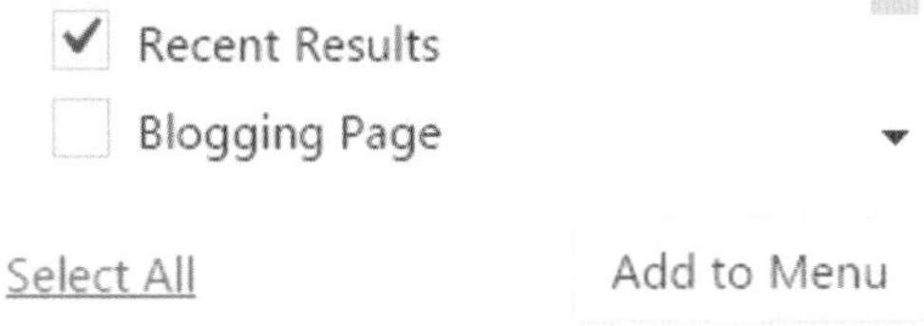

Pages ▼

Posts ▼

Lightbox Gallery ▼

Custom Links ▼

Categories ▼

Fig. 8.4 You can add most things to your menus.

✔ Recent Results

☐ Blogging Page ▼

Most Recent   View All

Select All   Add to Menu

Fig. 8.6 The selected page is added to the menu you are setting up.

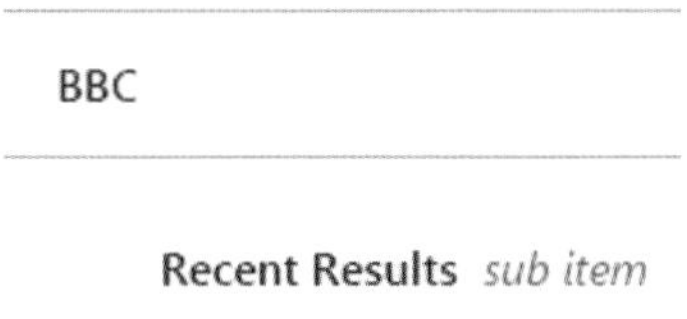

☐ Fascinating Fish
☐ Home
☐ No Access
☐ Membership Forms
☐ Fascinating Fish
☐ New Page
☐ Recent Results
☐ Blogging Page

BBC

Recent Results *sub item*

Fig. 8.7 The page make a sub item of the main menu entry.

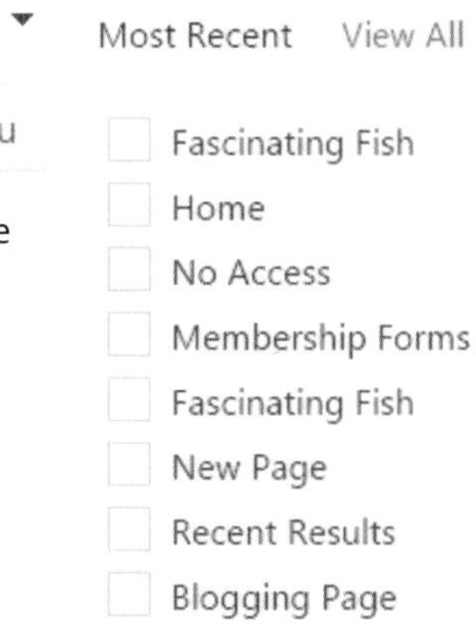

Fig. 8.5 A list of the most recent or you can opt for all pages.

Expand any of the   items by clicking on the down-facing arrowhead to see a list of recently created articles. Under the Pages entry is a list of recently created Pages (Figure 8.5).

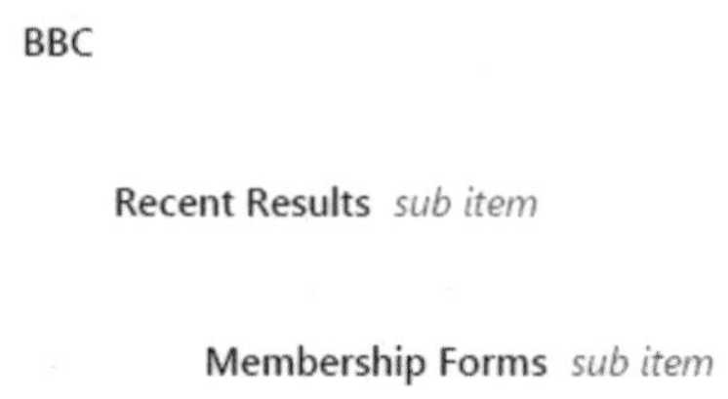

BBC
Recent Results sub item
Membership Forms sub item

Fig. 8.8 A menu nested two levels down and you can keep going down a few more.

BBC
Recent Results
Membership Forms

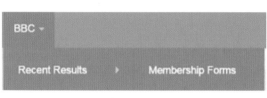

Fig. 8.9 The nested menus on the website. They open out in a downward direction and then expand horizontally. This will set a limit on how deeply you nest them.

Now select a page by ticking the box next to it and then the button **Add to Menu** (Figure 8.6). You will notice that the menu has added a top-level item. To make it a sub item drag and drop it onto the parent (Figure 8.7).

To create another level in your menus add the next item so it goes in as a top-level entry first of all and then drag and drop it onto the previous menu sub item. You now have the start of a nested menu system (Figure 8.8).

On the website the menu expands downwards and then sideways and is a compact way to provide lots of access to your information (Figure 8.9).

Plugins

As you might expect there are a large number of plugins associated with menus, nearly 1,500 at last count, with a focus on enhancing menus. I will just refer to one of them here to illustrate what is possible. Keep in mind that the plugin might not work with your theme or produce strange results.

The menu plugin I have selected is called Max Mega Menu Settings and it is full of features. As always the sequence is Install, Activate, read the documentation and apply it using the defaults until you understand what it can do.

Max Mega Menu Settings

Enable ✓

Event   Hover Intent ▼

Effect   Fade Up ▼   Fast ▼

Theme   Default ▼

Save

Fig. 8.10 You can make menus a bit better with the plugin. Experiment with the options to get an effect that you like.

Fig. 8.12 The theme viewer lets you know what will happen to your website on a mobile telephone.

This plugin adds another line in the Menu section above pages where there is a tick box to enable it. It is a two stage process of Saving the Menu Settings and then Saving the menu itself.

The menu previously styled to match the theme now has a style of its own (Figure 8.11) This is a good plugin as it opens up advanced styling features.

Fig. 8.11 New Style.

Mobile Devices and Special Menus

If you are building your website on a PC then the first thing to remember is to use a responsive theme. As the name implies, the theme detects the user's device and then adjusts the website to fit on the screen.

Figure 8.12 shows a website using the Hueman theme as it will be displayed on a mobile telephone. The theme may let you create a special menu for mobile users .

9

Completing Your WordPress Website

If you have followed the book in a more or less linear way then your website should be taking shape and probably has some content. It probably looks a bit ragged but this OK and nothing to worry about. Websites go through various changes as they get developed and then some more when the users give their feedback.

Professional developers use a number of techniques to design their websites. I want to introduce you to a couple of them but they share the common objective of getting a website looking right in the shortest possible time. They have fancy names but the concept behind them is quite useful to anyone creating a website.

Wireframing

This is a process of sketching out , it can be on paper or using a piece of software, each web page using blocks to designate menus, images, widgets and the number of columns of information on each page. I find that pencil, paper and eraser work as well as any software tool.

The sketches become your blueprint and you can tick off each area as you get it completed. It makes you disciplined in doing each task as there is a real risk of rushing in and changing settings at random, continually searching for better plugins and themes and so on.

I use this technique even if I am building the website for my own personal use. I spend a few hours away from the PC and tablet planning out each page. I also use the resulting plan as my task list and I tick things off as I configure WordPress. There does come a stage where I have a small snagging list to work through and time to look at improving the features on the website.

Rapid Application Development

RAD is one of many innovations in website and software development trying to get the end-user and the website builder to agree as quickly as possible on what the website should do and how it should look.

If you are working with a group of people there will always be one or two individuals who cannot visualise how the pages will look.

Having a set of sketches will help but at some point people will want to see something working. The idea behind RAD is that you create the main elements of the website but only about 5% of it actually works.

Say you have a menu with eight items then only the first one does anything. Widgets are in place but only one is configured. The website will have six pages but only one actually exists. I think you get the idea.

Development Website

I usually work with two copies of WordPress so that after one of them goes **live** I can try new plugins and themes out on the other one that is now the **test** website. Try not to put too much information on the test website otherwise Google might rank it higher than the live website. It does happen.

Robots.txt rewrite

Provide the easy managment of your robots.txt from admin side. It propose you the advanced then standard robots.txt content too.

By Eugen Bobrowski

Fig. 9.1 A useful plugin to control the search engines.

There is a plugin or two that you can use to tell Google, Bing and the other search engines not to crawl your website. There is a file titled robots.txt that contains the list of allowed and disallowed places that the crawlers can gather information.

The plugin shown in Figure 9.1 adds an entry to the Settings menu on the dashboard , Robots.txt Options, and by one simple action of setting the **Search Engine Visibility** to **Off** (Figure 9.2) the search engines will not add your content to their search indexes. They may gather it but they won't use it.

Search Engine Visibility

Fig. 9.2 An easy control for search engines

Keyboard Shortcuts

When using the in-built WordPress editor you can use a mouse or a combination of keys to edit and format the text.

Ctrl + a letter

On Windows and Linux use Ctrl key + a letter, on a Mac use Command key + a letter.

Letter	Action	Letter	Action
a	Select All	u	Underline text
b	Bold text	v	Paste
c	Copy	x	Cut
i	Italic text	y	Redo Action
k	Insert or edit link	z	Undo Action

Appendix 1—WordPress.com

If you consider yourself a novice when it comes to the internet and websites then going to **https://wordpress.com** and using their sign-up method might be just the solution you need. Space doesn't allow me to cover all the steps in detail but it is all pretty straightforward. WordPress soon detects your location and prices will be in your local currency.

Fig. 10.1 WordPress starting point.

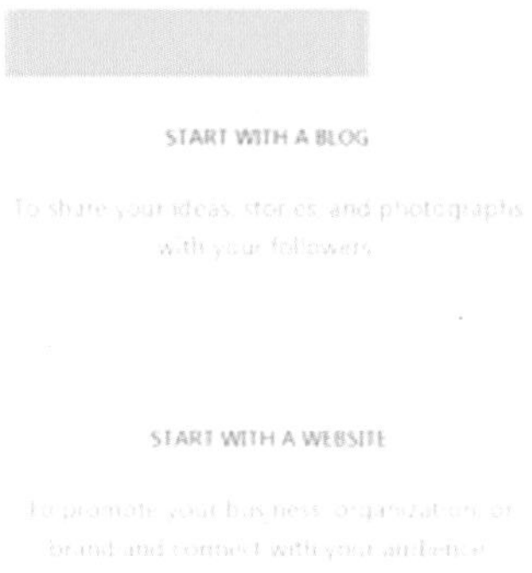

The WordPress.com website offers the user four options but we are only going to concern ourselves with two of them, a **blog** and a **website**. For reference, the other options are a **portfolio** site suitable for a photographer and an **online store**. The online store introduces several plugins that are beyond the scope of this book. Start with the website of your choice. WordPress may ask you to choose an industry sector for your website so that it can provide a choice of themes. Just pick the nearest industry.

Fig. 10.2 You will probably choose between a blog and a website.

I will guide you through some of the key steps that I went through to set up my **FREE** blog initially called **clubsoccer.wordpress.com**.

The website is a subdomain of WordPress.com. The website helpfully offers up alternative **domain names** that are not part of WordPress and encourages the buyer to upgrade to a paid-for product. (Figure 10.3). There is no need to do this just yet in case you decide that using WordPress is not for you. WordPress won't

Fig. 10.3 WordPress suggests a number of domain names that you might opt for instead of the free one that is an extension or subdomain of WordPress.com.

Fig. 10.4 You will need a unique user name.

give up easily and will remind you at nearly every stage to consider your own domain. Continue to select the FREE plan.

At the next step the administrator user id and password, also known as your credentials are set up and WordPress continues to prompt until a unique user name is provided. Once you clear all the error messages

Done! Thanks for waiting, we're ready for you to get started.

Fig. 10.5 The website is set up very quickly.

then you can click on **Create Account** (Figure 10.4). In just four steps you have created your new website. You just need to wait a bit for WordPress to be installed.

Within two minutes WordPress will be done and then clicking on **Continue** logs you into your very own WordPress website. That's it, you have a WordPress website

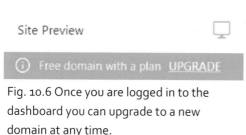

Fig. 10.6 Once you are logged in to the dashboard you can upgrade to a new domain at any time.

If you now want to have a domain of you own look on **Configure** and click on **Domain** to see the Upgrade message shown in Figure 10.6

Appendix 1A -The WordPress App

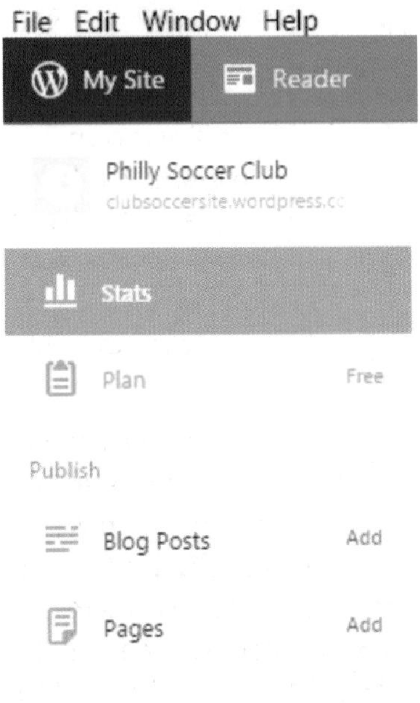

The WordPress app is available on the Google and Apple stores and is covered here for completeness as an alternative to a browser. The Windows version is called a desktop app and all the versions link up to websites hosted on WordPress.com and log administrators directly into that site as users use their administrator credentials to login into the app.

Fig. 10.7 The WordPress.com dashboard is a compact version of the usual dashboard implemented on other systems.

The **My Site** tab is used to access the dashboard of your own website and the **Reader** is to discover and follow other blogs hosted on WordPress.com.

The menus are compact and through them you can update both the website and your account with WordPress.

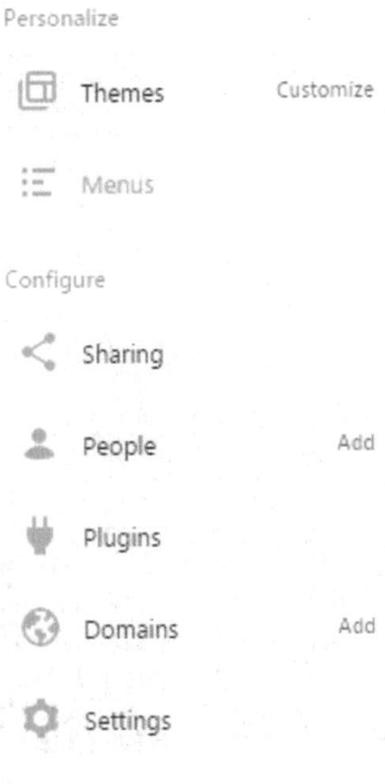

Fig. 10.8 The rest of the dashboard.

The app detects your local settings so prices for UK users are displayed in pounds rather than dollars. The app can also access

self-hosted sites and that means any website not hosted on the WordPress.com servers. If you have no plans to have more than one website then skip the rest of this section.

Look for the link on the app's sign in screen. It looks a bit complicated but it simply redirects you to the admin login for the website and allows you to install the **Jetpack** plugin that makes it possible.

The procedure is similar to the one for creating a website from scratch and you have to select a hosting plan. The best option is to select the free plan.

Fig. 10.9 The app sign-in is at the top and the instructions for adding another site below it.

Logout of WordPress.com when you complete all the steps otherwise you might end up in a confusing loop trying to find your website. When you log back in the website will be on the dashboard and if you have more than one website the menu bar will change from My Site to My Sites.

Jetpack Plugin

Jetpack is a plugin created by WordPress that provides a suite of tools to enhance your site. If you opted to use the WordPress.com hosted website then Jetpack is pre-installed and it is the only plugin allowed. WordPress includes the most popular plugins automatically. This is done so there is no chance of a user causing a server crash and it makes looking after the site a lot easier.

If you added your own website to the app then Jetpack is installed as a normal plugin and you have full control over your website. After you add your site an e-mail will appear in your inbox inviting you to learn more about it as it offers:

⇒   Malware scanning and removal

⇒   Daily or real-time backups

⇒   Industry-leading spam defence

⇒   Disaster recovery support.

Clicking on the **Learn More** link will open the login screen to your website. Alternatively login as the website administrator to install and activate the plugin. It only becomes clear when you activate this plugin that in addition to the features above Jetpack offers other useful tools:

⇒   Adds Twitter, Facebook and Google+ buttons to each post so visitors can share your content

⇒   Gives visitors two easy subscription options to notify them of new content

⇒   Adds a button to post and page editors, allowing you to build simple forms to help visitors stay in touch

⇒   Adds a carousel for your photos

⇒   Keeps visitors engaged on a blog by highlighting relevant content

⇒   Search Engine Optimisation (SEO) tools that have to be paid for.

Upgrading Your Plan

Upgrading to a new plan is easy and the information is readily available in your dashboard. The personal plan lets you pick a unique domain or custom name that will describe your website more accurately. Instead of relying on a forum where other users support you, WordPress offers live chat and e-mail support and in addition to more storage your website is also free of WordPress adverts.

The WordPress site will need a title and administrator credentials. You will also be given an option to add SSL to make it a secure website.

Appendix 2 - 1&1 WordPress

This appendix is a guide to using a hosting company , which is in business to sell space on their servers to individuals and businesses to create a website: on their servers you can install and configure your own WordPress based website.

There are many companies who do this and the process is similar no matter who you select. In addition to **1&1** , **123Reg** and **Godaddy** are recommended by many users.

Fig. 10.10 One of several companies offering a complete WordPress website as a package.

Use your browser to get to https:// www.1and1.co.uk and expand the Websites menu option to look at the options available for WordPress hosting. There are usually three levels, some on offer for the first year , and the **1&1 Managed WP Basic** will be more than adequate for most website users.

At the start you can elect to proceed without a domain and your website URL address will be something like **mylocalclubwebsite.apps-1and1-net**, which is not very memorable. If you know the domain name for your website enter it into the box and 1&1 will go through a process of checking that it is available or suggest alternatives. Some of these options, other than a co.uk based domain will add to your monthly cost.

You will get another chance later to change it to a more appropriate name. This is a good thing to do as it gives your website its unique identity.

During the setup process you will be offered many options to extend the duration of your contract which might make good sense for you to do and add other options around security features and search engines. For the most part you can ignore these enhancements unless you are a business.

The final thing to do at this stage is to create your 1&1 customer account and complete the payment stage. 1&1 will then send you several confirmation e-mails including one to access your site and setup WordPress.

Setting up WordPress

WordPress

The common publishing solution

✓ Easy installation and setup

✓ High flexibility with many plugins and themes

✓ Active Community

Fig. 10.11 You can get started straightaway on setting up your WordPress website.

Setting Up WordPress is straightforward and the key decision is to choose between a **Managed** installation or an **Unmanaged** one where you respond to updates and so on.

For a first time user of WordPress I definitely recommend going for the Managed option. You will need all your time for learning the package and for editing and creating content.

1&1 App Centre

WordPress Installation

Give your website a title

Website title

Fig. 10.12 You are taken to the App Centre but WordPress has been pre-selected for you. You just need a title for your website. You can change this later.

1&1 takes you through a number of steps to complete the basic setting up of a website. You are now in the 1&1 App Centre (Fig. 10.12)

Your website needs a title, so put in something meaningful. The text is accessible in the WordPress settings and can be changed later. Now create an admin user for WordPress (Fig. 10.13). Consider using different credentials to those for your 1&1 account for security reasons.

1&1 App Centre

WordPress Installation

Create a user for your website

Administrator login

Fig. 10.13 Create a login other than Admin for security reasons.

INSTALLED

Initially installed on: 03/03/17

⤴ Getting started with WordPress

Edit web site

Uninstall

Switch to Standard

Connect domain

Fig. 10.14 WordPress has been installed.

wpclublocation.co.uk   Connect domain

Fig. 10.15 Move or connect your temporary domain name to a more recognizable one.

Domain validated

SSL Starter

✓ Secures 1 domain

✓ Supports all popular browsers

✓ 256-bit SSL encryption

Fig. 10.16 Install SSL if you want. It may be a free add-on.

1&1 may now give you the option to confirm that you want to continue with a Managed WordPress website.

Accept this and move to the next stage. Soon you will see a message confirming that WordPress has been installed (Figure 10.14).

You are now nearing the end of the setup process with just one or two more choices to make.

If you didn't choose a conventional name for your website there is now an option to connect a new name to the internal 1&1 one as shown in Figure 10.15. This is a pre-requisite if you want to have a secure domain name. If not then you can proceed to edit your WordPress website.

If you want SSL then after you have set up your replacement domain name work through the SSL setup.

Using SSL gives your domain a **https://** prefix rather than a **http://** one . The reasons for using SSL are covered in Chapter 1 and if 1&1 are offering it for free then accept it.

Administering Your Website

The 1&1 WordPress is a fairly standard implementation that is not as restrictive as the WordPress.com version. Depending on your options the Admin login should be found at a URL like **https://wpclublocation.co.uk/wp-admin.**

Fig. 10.17 Look for this link.

Once the dashboard appears look on the menu for the 1&1 Wizard (Figure 10.17) and open it to select one of the five types of websites offered. You can use the wizard more than once to swap among them.

Configure WordPress

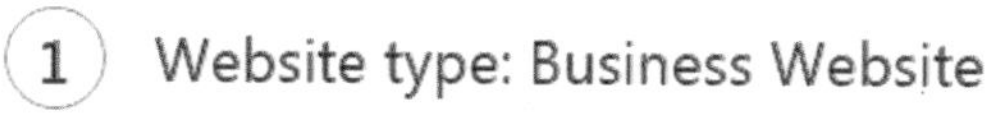

Fig. 10.18 Step 1: choose your website type.

Choose, for example, the Company option (Figure 10.18). The next step is selecting one of the six themes or add one of your own (Figure 10.19).

As a starter choose the one that visually looks like the best fit for your website that hopefully is based on a responsive design.

Fig. 10.19 Step 1: choose a design or theme.

The third stage is a set of recommended plugins, some of which are covered in the Plugins chapter in this book (Figure 10.20).

Fig. 10.20 Step 3: choose plugins or add-ons.

1&1 also has a recommendation for SEO or Search Engine Optimisation. The Yoast plugin is very well written but it is not for the novice user . Analytics are the third section and again best avoided unless you know what your are doing. The final section are miscellaneous plugins that you can come back to once you know some more about WordPress.

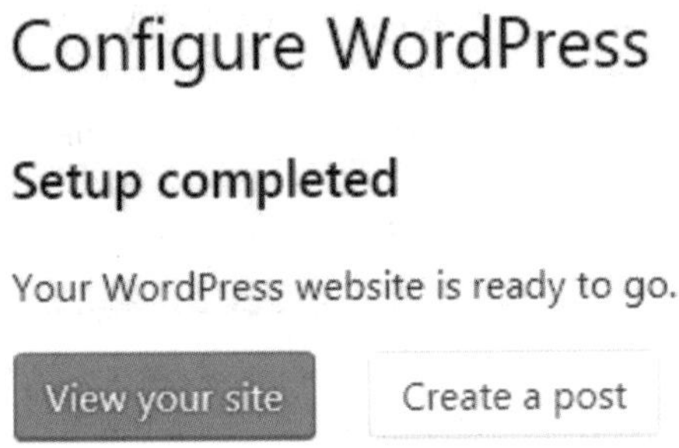

Configure WordPress

Setup completed

Your WordPress website is ready to go.

View your site   Create a post

Fig. 10.21 Job done. Look at your website or create your first post.

That's the basics done and now you can see the outcome of your selection or jump straight in to create your first post as shown in Figure 10.21.

Appendix 3 - CPanel Installation

Fig. 10.22 The cPanel logo is familiar to users who purchase web hosting space.

If you are using this option then you probably know your way around the control panel (Figure 10.22) provided by your web hosting company.

Softaculous Apps Installer

Fig. 10.23 Softaculous is a common application installer.

Most providers have a button or link to install common software packages such as WordPress, Joomla, and selected e-commerce and forum software. The choice and range is determined by the provider and several use Softaculous (Figure 10.23)

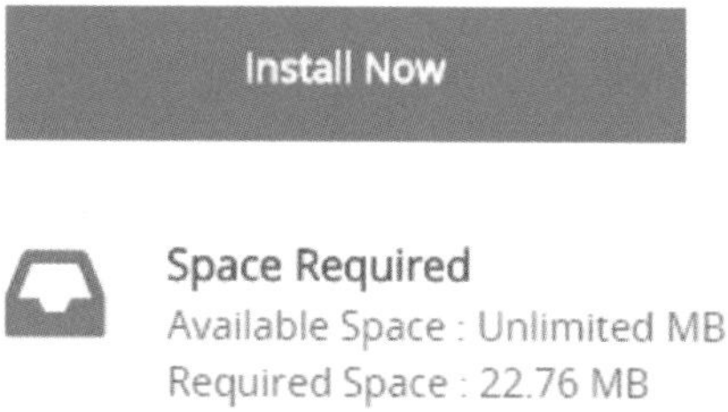

Install Now

Space Required
Available Space : Unlimited MB
Required Space : 22.76 MB

Fig. 10.24 The WordPress installer.

Others just list a few of the more popular ones. You will find WordPress listed under Blogs or CMS.

Select WordPress and click to Install it (Figure 10.24).

Carefully read the messages that appear on the screen as you may need to copy down login details and the URL to access the WordPress admin screen.

Do not assume that these details will be sent to you in an e-mail.

Appendix 4 - DNS Troubleshooting

If you have a problem finding your website in your browser and you get an error similar to Figure 10.25 it may be because the DNS server used by your broadband provider is updating very slowly.

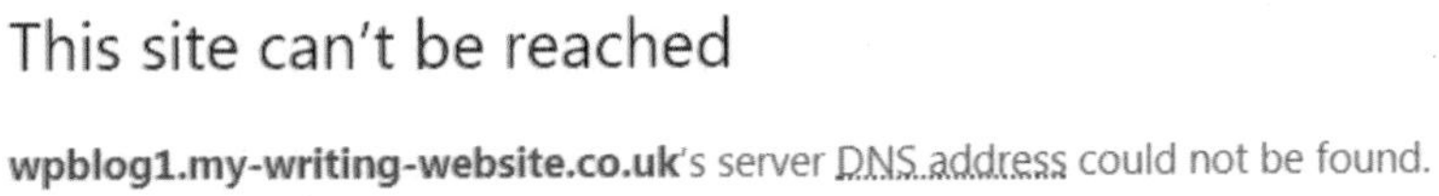

This site can't be reached
wpblog1.my-writing-website.co.uk's server DNS address could not be found.

Fig. 10.25 A simulated error message in Chrome.

You can either wait a few more days for any changes to work their way through the DNS server network or change the DNS your computer uses to convert your website's name into an IP address that your browser uses to reach the website.

I do not recommend changing the DNS server settings on your broadband router as this can cause many problems.

Google and OpenDNS are two very good public DNS server providers and both provide comprehensive instructions on how to change the DNS settings on your device.

Google

Google Public DNS
HOME
GUIDES
SUPPORT

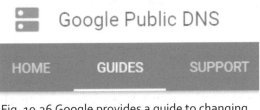

Fig. 10.26 Google provides a guide to changing the DNS servers on your device to theirs.

The URL for information on Windows, Apple and Android devices is found at:

https://developers.google.com/speed/public-dns/docs/using

OpenDNS

OpenDNS > OpenDNS Device Configuration

Fig. 10.27 The OpenDNS website has detailed information on operating systems and broadband routers.

Knowledge base

Windows 7   👍 84

OpenDNS Device Configuration > Computer Configuration

Fig. 10.28 You may have to search the OpenDNS site for your particular device or operating system.

If you find that the Google information is a bit too technical then go to the OpenDNS website where there are many diagrams to help you. The site tends to list current devices and if you are using Windows 7 then use the search tool on the site to obtain the instructions from the Knowledgebase.

Go to **https://support.opendns.com/hc/en-us** and click on the **OpenDNS Device Configuration** button.

Index

Index